Power Maths

Year 5 Textbook

M000035511

Series Editor: Tony Staneff

Dexter

Dexter is determined.

When he makes a mistake, he learns from it and tries again.

flexible

Flo

curious

Ash

brave

Astrid

helpful

Sparks

Pearson

Contents

Your teacher will tell you which page you need.

Unit 7 – Multiplication and division (2)   **6**

Multiplying numbers up to 4 digits by a 1-digit number   8

Multiplying 2-digit numbers (1)   12

Multiplying 2-digit numbers (2)   16

Multiplying 2-digit numbers (3)   20

Multiplying a 3-digit number by a 2-digit number   24

Multiplying a 4-digit number by a 2-digit number   28

Dividing up to a 4-digit number by a 1-digit number (1)   32

Dividing up to a 4-digit number by a 1-digit number (2)   36

Division with remainders (1)   40

Division with remainders (2)   44

Problem solving – division with remainders   48

End of unit check   52

Unit 8 – Fractions (1)   **54**

Equivalent fractions   56

Converting improper fractions to mixed numbers   60

Converting mixed numbers to improper fractions   64

Number sequences   68

Comparing and ordering fractions (1)   72

Comparing and ordering fractions (2)   76

Fractions as division (1)   80

Fractions as division (2)   84

End of unit check   88

Unit 9 – Fractions (2)   **90**

Adding and subtracting fractions with the same
denominator   92

Adding and subtracting fractions (1)   96

Adding and subtracting fractions (2)   100

Adding fractions (1)   104

Adding fractions (2)   108

Adding fractions (3)   112
Subtracting fractions (1)   116
Subtracting fractions (2)   120
Subtracting fractions (3)   124
Subtracting fractions (4)   128
Problem solving – mixed word problems (1)   132
Problem solving – mixed word problems (2)   136
End of unit check   140

Unit 10 – Fractions (3)   **142**
Multiplying fractions (1)   144
Multiplying fractions (2)   148
Multiplying fractions (3)   152
Multiplying fractions (4)   156
Calculating fractions of amounts   160
Using fractions as operators   164
Problem solving – mixed word problems   168
End of unit check   172

Unit 11 – Decimals and percentages   **174**
Writing decimals (1)   176
Writing decimals (2)   180
Decimals as fractions (1)   184
Decimals as fractions (2)   188
Understanding thousandths   192
Writing thousandths as decimals   196
Ordering and comparing decimals (1)   200
Ordering and comparing decimals (2)   204
Rounding decimals   208
Understanding percentages   212
Percentages as fractions and decimals   216
Equivalent fractions, decimals and percentages   220
End of unit check   224

What have we learnt?   232

Let's get started!

How to use this book

These pages make sure we're ready for the unit ahead. Find out what we'll be learning and brush up on your skills!

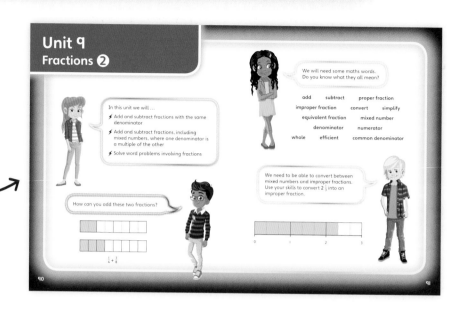

Discover

Lessons start with **Discover**.

Here, we explore new maths problems.

Can you work out how to find the answer?

Don't be afraid to make mistakes. Learn from them and try again!

Share

Next, we share our ideas with the class.

Did we all solve the problems the same way?
What ideas can you try?

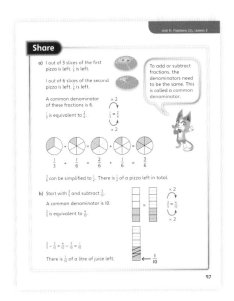

Think together

Then we have a go at some more problems together. Use what you have just learnt to help you.

We'll try a challenge too!

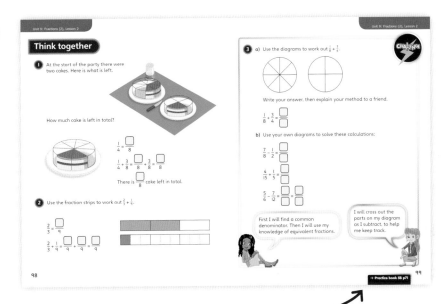

This tells you which page to go to in your **Practice Book**.

At the end of each unit there's an **End of unit check**. This is our chance to show how much we have learnt.

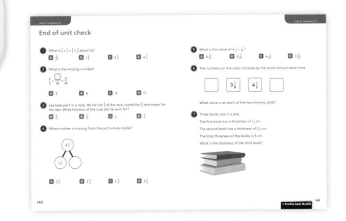

Unit 7
Multiplication and division ②

In this unit we will …

⚡ Multiply a number up to 4 digits by a 1- or 2-digit number

⚡ Divide a number up to 4 digits by a 1-digit number

⚡ Interpret remainders

⚡ Solve problems involving multiplication, division and remainders

How can you use the grid method to work out 17 × 4?

17

	10	7
4	10 × 4 = 40	7 × 4 = 28

```
  T  O
  4  0
+ 2  8
-------
  6  8
```

We will need some maths words.
Do you know what they all mean?

multiply   divide   add   subtract

place value   partition

equal   factor   multiple

remainder   sum   total

We also need to be able to
use the short division method.

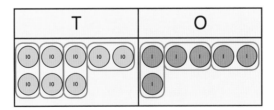

Multiplying numbers up to 4 digits by a 1-digit number

Discover

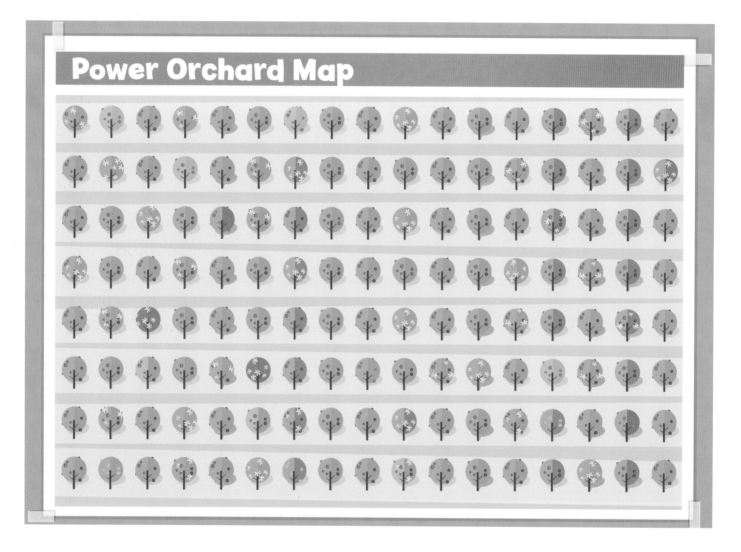

Power Orchard Map

1 **a)** How many trees are there in total?

  b) A group of children pick 6 apples from each tree.

  How many apples do they pick altogether?

Share

a) There are 8 rows of trees, with 17 trees in each row.

Method 1

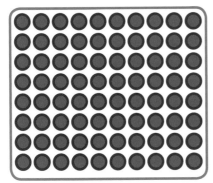

$8 \times 10 = 80$

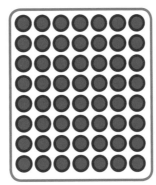

$8 \times 7 = 56$

$80 + 56 = 136$

I used counters to represent the trees. I partitioned the counters into sections to make it easier for me to work out the total.

Method 2

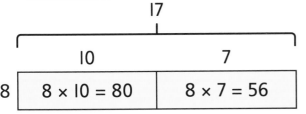

	17	
	10	7
8	$8 \times 10 = 80$	$8 \times 7 = 56$

```
  H   T   O
      8   0
+     5   6
─────────────
  1   3   6
```

My method works a bit like yours. It is called the grid method.

Method 3

```
      1   7
×         8
─────────────
  1   3   6
        5
```

I used the column method that we did last year. This is called short multiplication.

Method 4

$17 \times 8 = 10 \times 8 + 7 \times 8$

$ = 80 + 56$

$ = 136$

There are 136 trees in total.

b) There are 136 trees and the children pick 6 apples from each tree.

Multiply 136 × 6 to find how many apples they pick altogether.

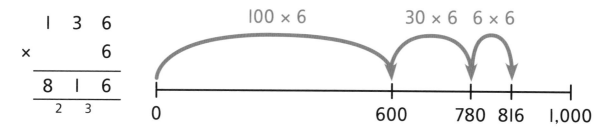

```
    1  3  6
  ×       6
  _____
    8  1  6
       2  3
```

The children pick 816 apples altogether.

Think together

1 What multiplication does each of these models show?

Work out the answer to each multiplication.

a)

	100	60	3
5	100 × 5 = 500	60 × 5 = 300	3 × 5 = 15

$\square$ × $\square$ = $\square$

b)

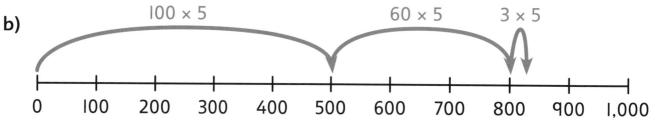

$\square$ × $\square$ = $\square$

c)

H	T	O
(100)	(10)(10)(10)(10)(10) (10)	(1)(1)(1)
(100)	(10)(10)(10)(10)(10) (10)	(1)(1)(1)
(100)	(10)(10)(10)(10)(10) (10)	(1)(1)(1)
(100)	(10)(10)(10)(10)(10) (10)	(1)(1)(1)
(100)	(10)(10)(10)(10)(10) (10)	(1)(1)(1)

$\square$ × $\square$ = $\square$

2 Fill in the missing numbers to complete the multiplications.

a) $42 \times 7 = \boxed{}$

```
    4  2
  ×    7
  _____

  _____
```

b) $142 \times 7 = \boxed{}$

```
   1  4  2
  ×     7
  _____

  _____
```

c) $3,142 \times 7 = \boxed{}$

```
   3  1  4  2
  ×        7
  _____

  _____
```

CHALLENGE

3 Danny and Zac are representing calculations using bar models.

What calculations are being represented? Work out the answers.

a)

Danny

| ? |
| 3,285 | 3,285 | 3,285 |

b)

Zac

| 329 | 329 | 329 | 329 | 329 | 329 |

| 658 | 658 | 658 | 658 | 658 |

?

 To work out Zac's calculation, I think I need to do two multiplications.

I think I can do it as just one multiplication.

11

Multiplying 2-digit numbers ❶

Discover

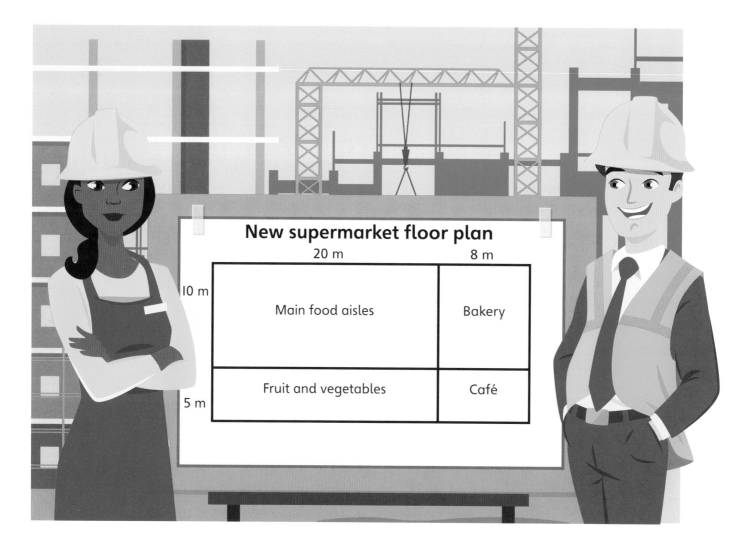

New supermarket floor plan

	20 m	8 m
10 m	Main food aisles	Bakery
5 m	Fruit and vegetables	Café

❶ **a)** What will the length of the new supermarket be?

What will the width be?

b) What will the total area of the new supermarket be?

Share

a)

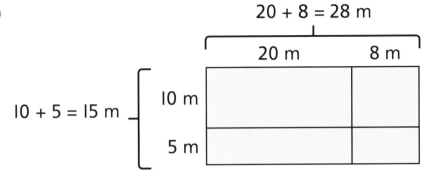

$20 + 8 = 28$ m

$10 + 5 = 15$ m

10 m

5 m

20 m   8 m

The length of the new supermarket will be 28 m.

The width will be 15 m.

b)

> To find the total area I need to work out 28×15 but I am not sure how to do that.

> The area model looks like the grid method. I will find the area of each part of the supermarket and add them together to get the total area.

	20 m	8 m
10 m	$20 \times 10 = 200$ m^2	$8 \times 10 = 80$ m^2
5 m	$20 \times 5 = 100$ m^2	$8 \times 5 = 40$ m^2

H	T	O
2	0	0
1	0	0
	8	0
+	4	0
4	2	0
	1	

The total area of the new supermarket will be 420 m^2.

This is the same as 28×15.

13

Think together

1) This is the floor plan for a new toy shop.

30 m	7 m

20 m

Crafts

$30 \times 20 = \boxed{}$ m²

Bikes

$7 \times \boxed{} = \boxed{}$ m²

3 m

Toys

$\boxed{} \times \boxed{} = \boxed{}$ m²

Board games

$\boxed{} \times \boxed{} = \boxed{}$ m²

a) Find the area of each section in the new toy shop.

The area of the Crafts section is $\boxed{}$ m².

The area of the Bikes section is $\boxed{}$ m².

The area of the Toys section is $\boxed{}$ m².

The area of the Board games section is $\boxed{}$ m².

b) What is the total area of the new toy shop?

H T O

+
_____

_____

The total area of the toy shop is $\boxed{}$ m².

2 Use the area model to work out 52 × 18.

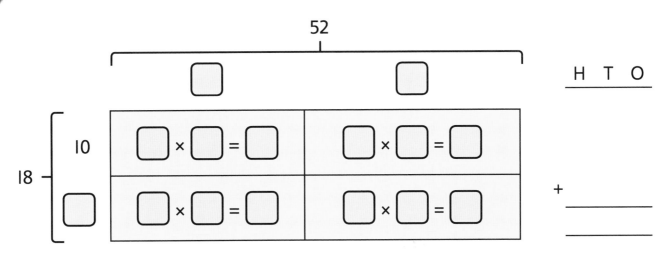

H T O

+
_____
_____

52 × 18 = ☐

3 **a)** Draw an area model to work out each of these calculations.

CHALLENGE

45 × 37   29 × 81 38^2

The boxes in your area models do not need to be exactly to scale. They do need to be big enough to write in the calculations.

b) Max says that the answer to 34 × 18 is 594.

How do you know that Max is not correct just by looking at the last digits in the multiplication?

15

Multiplying 2-digit numbers ②

Discover

Today I have 10 green crates of milk, 10 blue crates and 3 red crates to deliver.

① **a)** Each crate contains 15 bottles of milk. Find the total number of bottles by working out how many bottles are in each of the different coloured crates.

b) Work out 23 × 15.

Share

a)

$10 \times 15 = 150$

$10 \times 15 = 150$

	H	T	O
	1	5	0
	1	5	0
+		4	5
	3	4	5
		1	

$3 \times 15 = 45$

There are 345 bottles of milk in total.

b) Method 1

	20	3
10	$20 \times 10 = 200$	$3 \times 10 = 30$
5	$20 \times 5 = 100$	$3 \times 5 = 15$

	H	T	O
	2	0	0
	1	0	0
		3	0
+		1	5
	3	4	5

Method 2

	23
10	$23 \times 10 = 230$
5	$23 \times 5 = 115$

	H	T	O
	2	3	0
+	1	1	5
	3	4	5

I partitioned 23 and 15.

I decided not to partition 23. I can just multiply 23 by 10 and 5.

$23 \times 15 = 23 \times 10 + 23 \times 5 = 230 + 115 = 345$

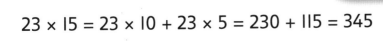

Method 3

$23 \times 15 = 10 \times 15 + 10 \times 15 + 3 \times 15$

$\qquad = \quad 150 \quad + \quad 150 \quad + \quad 45$

$\qquad = 345$

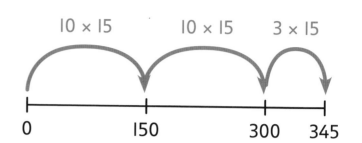

I can think of other ways to partition these numbers.

You can partition the number in other ways, like this for example.

$23 \times 15 = 20 \times 15 + 3 \times 15$

$\qquad = 300 \quad + \quad 45$

$\qquad = 345$

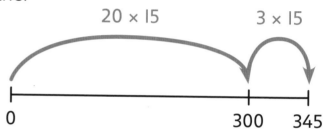

Think together

1 Each box contains 12 rulers. How many rulers are there in total?

$27 \times 12 = 10 \times \boxed{} + 10 \times \boxed{} + \boxed{} \times \boxed{}$

$\qquad = \boxed{} + \boxed{} + \boxed{}$

$\qquad = \boxed{}$

There are $\boxed{}$ rulers in total.

2 Mrs Dean has 24 tubs of drawing pins. Each tub contains 36 pins.

How many pins does she have in total?

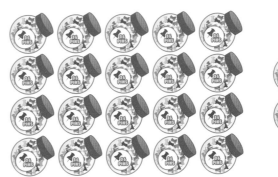 

```
        20              4
   ┌───────────┬───────────┐
36 │           │           │
   └───────────┴───────────┘
```

24 × 36 = ☐ × 36 + ☐ × 36

= ☐ + ☐

= ☐

She has ☐ pins in total.

3

a) Use partitioning to work out 26 × 18.

b) Danny does these calculations to work out the answer to a multiplication.

CHALLENGE

```
                              H  T  O
                              3  9  0
   30 × 13 = 390        1  3  +  1  1  7
                    ×      9  ────────
                    ────────  5  0  7
                    1  1  7      1
                       2
```

What two 2-digit numbers is Danny multiplying together?

19

Multiplying 2-digit numbers ❸

Discover

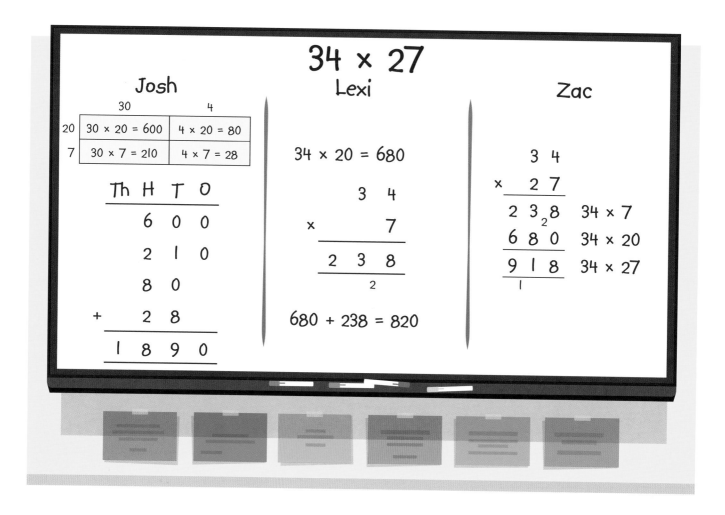

 a) What mistake has Josh made?

b) Look at Lexi's method and Zac's method.

What is the same? What is different?

Share

a) The calculations in the grid are all correct but Josh has lined up the numbers incorrectly in his addition.

	30	4
20	30 × 20 = 600	4 × 20 = 80
7	30 × 7 = 210	4 × 7 = 28

```
Th  H  T  O
    6  0  0
    2  1  0
       8  0
+      2  8
    9  1  8
       1
```

The correct answer is 918.

b) Lexi partitioned her number and worked out each multiplication separately.

Lexi did that correctly, but she then made a mistake when adding her two totals.

Zac did the same as Lexi, except he did it all in one column multiplication and made no mistakes. This is called long multiplication.

34 × 20 = 680

```
    3  4
×      7
    2  3  8
       2
```

```
    3  4
×   2  7
  2  3 ₂8   34 × 7
```

```
    3  4
×   2  7
  2  3 ₂8   34 × 7
  6  8  0   34 × 20
```

```
    3  4
×   2  7
  2  3 ₂8   34 × 7
  6  8  0   34 × 20
  9  1  8   34 × 27
       1
```

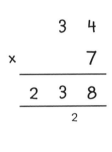

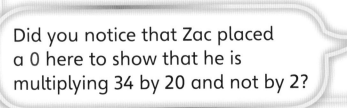

Did you notice that Zac placed a 0 here to show that he is multiplying 34 by 20 and not by 2?

Think together

1 Mr Jones sets the class some more long multiplication questions.

Complete each multiplication.

a) 46 × 13

```
        4   6
  ×     1   3
  _____
          , 8      46 × 3
          1
            0      46 × 10
  _____
            8      46 × 13
  _____
```

b) 34 × 24

```
        3   4
  ×     2   4
  _____
                   34 × 4
            0      34 × 20
  _____
                   34 × 24
  _____
```

c) 37 × 21

```
        3   7
  ×     2   1
  _____
                   37 × 1
            0      37 × 20
  _____
                   37 × 21
  _____
```

2 Mr Jones's class are going on a school trip.

There are 29 children in the class and they each pay £15.

How much money is paid in total by all the children?

£ ⬚ is paid in total.

3 **a)** Josh works out 63 × 24.

```
        6  3
×       2  4
────────────
     2  4  1  2
     1  2  6  0
────────────
     3  6  7  2
────────────
```

What mistake has Josh made?

Show the correct long multiplication.

b) Zac has worked out another multiplication.

What two numbers has Zac multiplied together?

```
×      ✳  ✳
       ✳  ✳
────────────
    3  8 ₂ 7
    4  3  0
────────────
    8  1  7
       ₁
```

> I will think about what two numbers multiply together to make 27 first.

→ **Practice book 5B p15**

Multiplying a 3-digit number by a 2-digit number

Discover

These 143 packs are for the local supermarket.

100 packs

40 packs

1 pack

1 pack

1 pack

12 boxes = 1 pack

1 **a)** How many boxes of cereal are there in 143 packs?

   Use the grid method to work out the answer.

   b) Check your answer using long multiplication.

Share

a) There are 12 boxes of cereal in each pack.

	100	40	3
10	100 × 10 = 1,000	40 × 10 = 400	3 × 10 = 30
2	100 × 2 = 200	40 × 2 = 80	3 × 2 = 6

	Th	H	T	O
	1	0	0	0
		4	0	0
		2	0	0
			8	0
			3	0
+				6
	1	7	1	6
			1	

143 × 12 = 1,716

There are 1,716 boxes of cereal in total.

b) You can extend the long multiplication from last time.

```
      1  4  3
  ×      1  2
  ─────────────
      2  8  6     143 × 2
   1  4  3  0     143 × 10
   1  7  1  6     143 × 12
         1
```

> First, I multiplied each digit in the 3-digit number by 2.
>
> Then I multiplied each digit by 10. To do this I put in the 0 and then multiplied each digit by 1.

143 × 12 = 1,716

So, the answer found with the grid method is correct.

Think together

1. Mega Flakes also makes larger packs that each contain 16 boxes of cereal.

A supermarket buys 217 of these packs.

1 pack

16 boxes = 1 pack

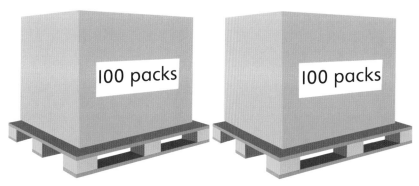

100 packs   100 packs

10 packs

1 pack 1 pack
1 pack 1 pack
1 pack 1 pack
1 pack 1 pack

How many boxes of cereal does this supermarket buy in total?

Work it out using the grid method and long multiplication.

Grid method:

	200	10	7
10			
6			

```
   H  T  O
   _____



+  _____

   _____
```

Long multiplication:

```
      2  1  7
   ×     1  6
   _____
         ₄2
         0
```

This supermarket buys ☐ boxes of cereal in total.

26

2 Complete these multiplications.

a) 263 × 32 = ☐

```
    2  6  3
×      3  2
_____
                263 × 2
                263 × 30
_____     263 × 32
```

b) 520 × 26 = ☐

```
    5  2  0
×      2  6
_____
                520 × 6
                520 × 20
_____     520 × 26
```

3 Mo has five digit cards.

```
[ 1 ]  [ 3 ]  [ 5 ]  [ 7 ]  [ q ]
```

He uses the cards to make a 2-digit number and a 3-digit number and then multiplies them together.

```
[ 1 ][ 5 ]        [ 3 ][ q ][ 7 ]
```

a) What answer should Mo get?

b) Rearrange the cards to make a multiplication with a bigger answer. Is there a multiplication that gives a smaller answer?

> I am just going to try some numbers and see how big an answer I get.

> I will write the 3-digit number above the 2-digit number for my multiplications.

27

Multiplying a 4-digit number by a 2-digit number

Discover

1 a) There are 1,274 adults watching the show.

How much money has been made from adult tickets?

b) All the seats have been filled.

How much money has been made from child tickets?

Share

a) An adult ticket costs £32.

1,274 adult tickets were sold.

I multiplied 1,274 by 32 to find the total amount.

First multiply 1,274 by 2.

```
    1  2  7  4
×         3  2
─────────────
    2  5₁ 4  8     1,274 × 2
─────────────
─────────────
```

Then multiply 1,274 by 30.

```
      1  2  7  4
×           3  2
───────────────
      2  5₁ 4  8     1,274 × 2
    3  8₂ 2₁ 2  0     1,274 × 30
───────────────
```

We put down the 0 and multiply each digit by 3.

Finally add up the numbers.

```
    1  2  7  4
×         3  2
─────────────
    2  5₁ 4  8     1,274 × 2
  3  8₂ 2₁ 2  0     1,274 × 30
─────────────
  4  0  7  6  8     1,274 × 32
─────────────
     ₁
```

I was going to use the grid method, but this seems much quicker.

£40,768 has been made from adult tickets.

b) There are 1,659 people watching the show in total.

1,274 of these people are adults.

1,659	
1,274	385

```
   1  ⁵8̸ ¹5  9
 -  1  2  7  4
       3  8  5
```

There are 385 children watching the show.

A child ticket costs £19.

```
        3  8  5
  ×        1  9
     3  4₇ 6₄ 5
     3  8  5  0
     7  3  1  5
        |     |
```

£7,315 has been made from child tickets.

Think together

1 Complete these long multiplications.

a) 1,226 × 21

```
    1  2  2  6
  ×        2  1
  _____
```

b) 3,405 × 35

```
    3  4  0  5
  ×        3  5
  _____
```

2 A plane flies from London to Rome and back again twice a day.

The distance of the flight from London to Rome is 1,445 km.

How far does the plane travel in 25 days?

The plane travels ⬜ km in 25 days.

3 Fill in the missing digits.

a)

```
        7  ✱
  ×     1  6
     4  ✱  0
     7  ✱  0
  1  ✱  ✱  0
```

b)

```
     ✱  4  ✱  9
  ×        3  6
  ✱  ✱  4  5  ✱
  7  ✱  ✱  ✱  0
  ✱  ✱  ✱  ✱  4
```

I need to use the second line of calculation in b) to work out how many thousands are in the top number.

31

→ Practice book 5B p21

Dividing up to a 4-digit number by a 1-digit number ①

Discover

FAIR
RIDE TICKET PRICES
Single ticket: 50p
Book of 10 tickets: £4
Firework display, 7 pm each day!!

Roller coaster: 4 people per car

We've got 64 tickets to share between our 2 classes.

Miss Hall   Mr Lopez

① **a)** Mr Lopez and Miss Hall share the 64 tickets equally.

How many tickets does each class get?

b) There are 48 children at the fair. They all go on the roller coaster together.

How many cars will they need in total?

Share

a) The 64 tickets are shared between 2 classes.

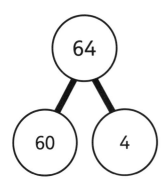

$60 \div 2 = 30$

$4 \div 2 = 2$

$30 + 2 = 32$

$64 \div 2 = 32$, so each class gets 32 tickets.

b) There are 48 children. 4 children can sit in each car.

So, you need to divide 48 by 4. There are two ways of doing this.

I used multiplication facts to solve the division. I knew that $4 \times 12 = 48$ so $48 \div 4 = 12$.

Method 1

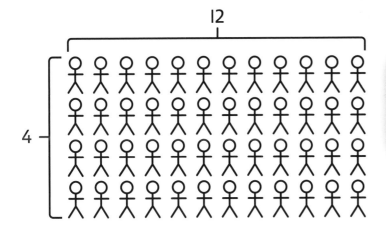

I grouped the children into columns of 4 and counted the number of columns.

Method 2

I used a method called short division.

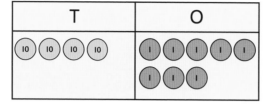

Lay out the problem as a short division, like this.

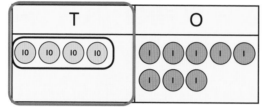

There is 1 group of 4 in 4 tens.

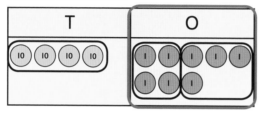

There are 2 groups of 4 in 8 ones.

$48 ÷ 4 = 12$

They will need 12 cars in total.

Think together

 1 96 pens are shared equally between 3 classes.

How many pens does each class receive?

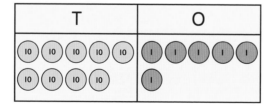

Each class receives ☐ pens.

2 Complete these divisions.

a) 428 ÷ 2 = ☐

2 | 4 2 8

H	T	O
100 100 100 100	10 10	1 1 1 1 1 1 1 1

b) 9,636 ÷ 3 = ☐

3 | 9 6 3 6

Th	H	T	O
1,000 1,000 1,000 1,000 1,000 1,000 1,000 1,000 1,000	100 100 100 100 100 100	10 10 10	1 1 1 1 1 1

3 Over 3 nights, 609 fireworks are set off at the fair. An equal number is set off each night.

The owner of the fair wants to work out how many fireworks were used each night. The owner does this division.

$$\begin{array}{r} 2\ 3 \\ 3\,\overline{|\,6\ 0\ 9} \end{array}$$

Is the owner correct? Explain your answer.

> I think he is right. I think you just need to put a zero at the end, so he needs 230 fireworks.

> Are you sure? I can use multiplication to check if he is correct.

35

→ Practice book 5B p24

Dividing up to a 4-digit number by a 1-digit number ❷

Discover

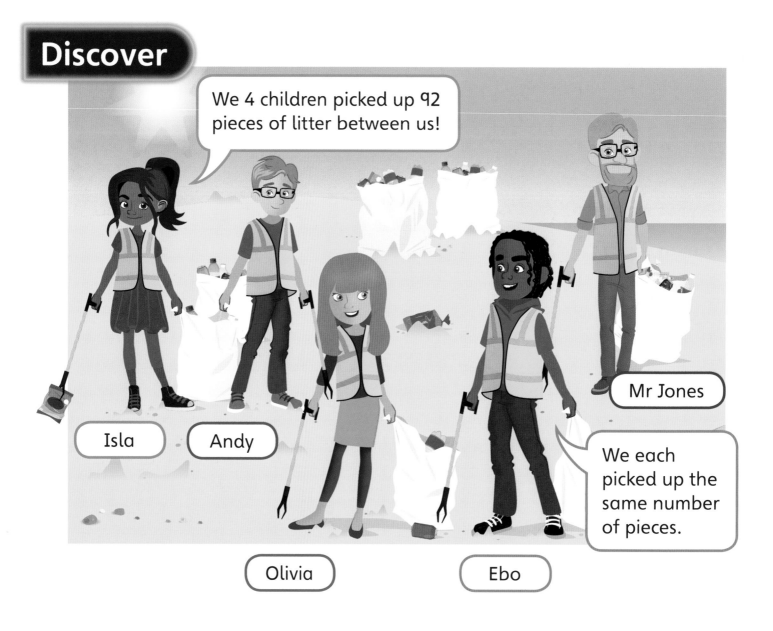

1 **a)** How many pieces of litter has each child picked up?

b) Mr Jones has picked up 351 pieces of litter. He shares them equally between 3 bags.

How many pieces of litter are in each bag?

Share

a) 4 children picked up 92 pieces of litter.

They each picked up the same number of pieces.

To work this out, I need to divide 92 by 4. I will use the method of short division that we learnt in the last lesson.

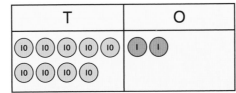

First, lay out the problem.

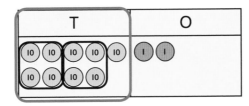

How many groups of 4 go into 9 tens?

2 groups of 4 tens with 1 ten left over.

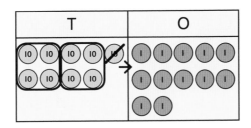

Exchange the 1 ten left over for 10 ones.

We now have 12 ones.

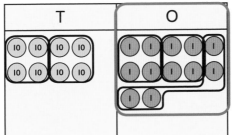

How many groups of 4 go into 12 ones?

3 groups of 4 ones.

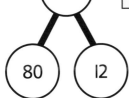

I used a part-whole model to partition the number into two numbers that divide by 4.

80 ÷ 4 = 20   12 ÷ 4 = 3

20 + 3 = 23

92 ÷ 4 = 23, so each child picked up 23 pieces of litter.

b) Mr Jones shares 351 pieces of litter equally between 3 bags.

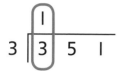

There is 1 group of 3 hundreds.

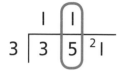

There is 1 group of 3 tens and 2 tens left over.

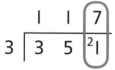
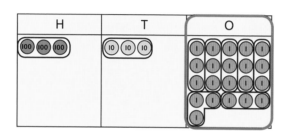

Exchange the 2 tens for 20 ones. You now have 21 ones

There are 7 groups of 3 ones in 21.

$351 \div 3 = 117$

There are 117 pieces of litter in each bag.

Think together

1 The children have a flask containing 575 ml of juice.

They share the juice equally among themselves and Mr Jones.

How much juice does each person get?

$575 \div 5 = \boxed{}$

Each person gets $\boxed{}$ ml of juice.

H	T	O
100 100 100 100 100	10 10 10 10 10 10 10	1 1 1 1 1

2 Complete these short divisions.

a) 726 ÷ 6 = ☐

$6 \overline{\smash{\big)}\ 7\ 2\ 6}$

H	T	O
100 100 100 100 100 100 100	10 10	1 1 1 1 1 1

b) 522 ÷ 3 = ☐

$3 \overline{\smash{\big)}\ 5\ 2\ 2}$

H	T	O
100 100 100 100 100	10 10	1 1

3 a) Look at these division problems.

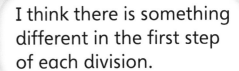

> There are 312 eggs. How many boxes of 6 eggs can be made?

> Divide 1,980 by 2

> 475 ÷ 5

What is different about these divisions compared with the ones you have been doing so far?

I think there is something different in the first step of each division.

b) Max tries to work out the third division problem. What mistake has Max made?

$5 \overline{\smash{\big)}\ 4\ {}^1 7\ {}^2 5}$ with 0 3 5 above

39

Division with remainders ❶

Discover

Holly

Each tray holds 6 cake cases.

We need to put the cake cases into the trays.

Lee

Lexi

80 cake cases

❶ **a)** How many full trays of cakes can be made?

Will there be any cake cases left over?

Use a method other than short division to find your answer.

b) Check your answer using short division.

Share

I put 80 counters into groups of 6.

a) Method 1

13 full trays

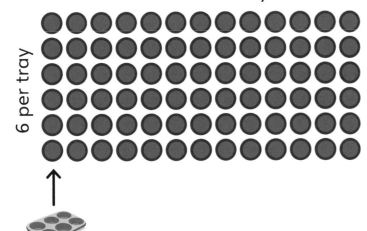

6 per tray

 2 left over

Remember the amount left over is called the remainder.

We use the letter r to represent remainder.

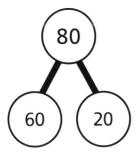

$80 \div 6 = 13 \text{ r } 2$

There are 13 full trays and 2 cake cases left over.

Method 2

$3 \times 6 = 18$ $10 \times 6 = 60$

0 2   20   80

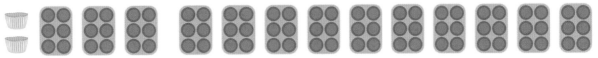

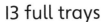

80

60   20

$60 \div 6 = 10$

$20 \div 6 = 3 \text{ r } 2$

So, $80 \div 6 = 13 \text{ r } 2$

I used a part-whole model to help me.

b)

6 | 8 0

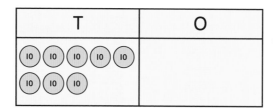

Lay out the problem as short division.

$$\begin{array}{c} 1 \\ 6\,|\,8\,^20 \end{array}$$

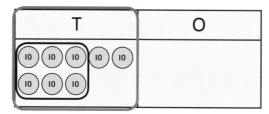

How many groups of 6 go into 8 tens?

There is 1 group of 6 tens.

There are 2 tens remaining.

$$\begin{array}{c} 1\quad3\ \text{r}\,2 \\ 6\,|\,8\,^20 \end{array}$$

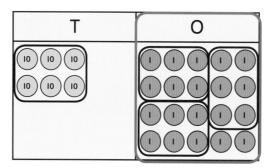

How many groups of 6 go into 20 ones?

There are 3 groups of 6 ones.

There are 2 ones remaining.

There are 13 full trays and 2 cake cases left over.

Think together

1 Lexi wants to share the 80 cakes equally between the 3 storage tins.

Will she be able to do this?

3 | 8 0

T	O
10 10 10 10 10 10 10 10	

2 Work out these short divisions.

a) $97 \div 7 =$ ☐ r ☐

$7 \overline{)9\ 7}$

T	O
10 10 10 10 10 10 10 10 10	1 1 1 1 1 1 1

b) $173 \div 4 =$ ☐ r ☐

$4 \overline{)1\ 7\ 3}$

H	T	O
100	10 10 10 10 10 10 10	1 1 1

CHALLENGE

3 a) Predict which of these divisions will have a remainder.

$95 \div 5$ $191 \div 2$ $535 \div 4$

Check using the short division method.

How accurate were your predictions?

b) Is it possible to work out the remainders to these divisions, even though some of the numbers are unknown?

?6 ÷ 5   7?3 ÷ 2

???6 ÷ 5   73? ÷ 2

I think I will use my knowledge of the 2 and 5 times-tables to help me.

43

→ Practice book 5B p30

Division with remainders ❷

Discover

We have 253 slices of pizza left to sell today.

1 **a)** 6 slices make one whole pizza.

How do you know that the 253 slices will not make a whole number of pizzas with no spare slices left over?

b) How many whole pizzas can the chefs make?

What fraction of a pizza will be left over?

Share

a) We need to find out if 253 can divide exactly by 6.

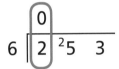

1	2	3	4	5	6	7	8	9	10
11	12	13	14	15	16	17	18	19	20
21	22	23	24	25	26	27	28	29	30
31	32	33	34	35	36	37	38	39	40
41	42	43	44	45	46	47	48	49	50
51	52	53	54	55	56	57	58	59	60
61	62	63	64	65	66	67	68	69	70
71	72	73	74	75	76	77	78	79	80
81	82	83	84	85	86	87	88	89	90
91	92	93	94	95	96	97	98	99	100

I marked all the multiples of 6 on a 100 square. I noticed that they are all even numbers.

6 is a multiple of 2 and 3, so a number that is a multiple of 6 is also a multiple of 2 and 3.

253 is not an even number, so it is not a multiple of 2.

253 cannot divide exactly by 6. There will be some slices of pizza left over.

b)

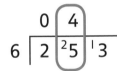

$$6 \overline{\smash{)}2 \,^2 5 \quad 3}$$

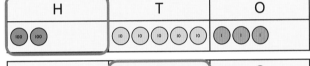

H	T	O

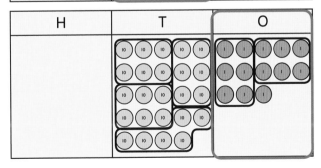

The chefs can make 42 whole pizzas.

There is 1 slice left over. 1 slice is $\frac{1}{6}$ of a pizza.

45

Think together

1 1,350 grams of flour is divided equally between 5 bowls.

a) How do you know that 1,350 divides exactly by 5?

1	2	3	4	5	6	7	8	9	10
11	12	13	14	15	16	17	18	19	20
21	22	23	24	25	26	27	28	29	30
31	32	33	34	35	36	37	38	39	40
41	42	43	44	45	46	47	48	49	50

b) How much flour goes into each bowl?

$$5 \overline{)1\ 3\ 5\ 0}$$

Th	H	T	O
1,000	100 100 100	10 10 10 10 10	

☐ g of flour goes into each bowl.

2 What is the remainder in each of these divisions?

575 ÷ 5	137 ÷ 2	140 ÷ 7
576 ÷ 5	138 ÷ 2	142 ÷ 7
577 ÷ 5	139 ÷ 2	145 ÷ 7
579 ÷ 5	140 ÷ 2	1,401 ÷ 7

I wonder if I can work out some of these without doing the division.

3 **a)** Put counters on all the numbers that are multiples of 3.

Pick one of the numbers that has a counter on it and add the digits together.

Repeat this two more times.
What do you notice?

1	2	3	4	5	6	7	8	9	10
11	12	13	14	15	16	17	18	19	20
21	22	23	24	25	26	27	28	29	30
31	32	33	34	35	36	37	38	39	40
41	42	43	44	45	46	47	48	49	50
51	52	53	54	55	56	57	58	59	60
61	62	63	64	65	66	67	68	69	70
71	72	73	74	75	76	77	78	79	80
81	82	83	84	85	86	87	88	89	90
91	92	93	94	95	96	97	98	99	100

b) Use this to decide if each of these numbers divides exactly by 3.

729   111   715   1,651   2,538

I will add up the digits of each number to help me. I remember that this is called the digit sum.

I think all the digit sums for numbers that divide exactly by 3 are multiples of the same number.

How can you work out the remainder without doing the division?

47

Problem solving – division with remainders

Discover

Rearrange the digits to make your own 3-digit number.

Now tell me a division fact about your number.

When you divide my number by 4, you get 153 r 3.

My number is a multiple of 6.

5 6 1

Miss Hall

Reena   Kate   Richard   Zac

① **a)** What number could Zac have made?

How many possible numbers can you find?

b) What number did Reena make?

Share

a)

◯ are multiples of 2.

▨ are multiples of 3.

> I know that numbers that are multiples of 6 are also multiples of 2 and 3.

1	2	3	4	5	6	7	8	9	10
11	12	13	14	15	16	17	18	19	20
21	22	23	24	25	26	27	28	29	30
31	32	33	34	35	36	37	38	39	40
41	42	43	44	45	46	47	48	49	50
51	52	53	54	55	56	57	58	59	60
61	62	63	64	65	66	67	68	69	70
71	72	73	74	75	76	77	78	79	80
81	82	83	84	85	86	87	88	89	90
91	92	93	94	95	96	97	98	99	100

> I remember a rule to find out if a number divides exactly by 3.

The digits 5, 6 and 1 add up to 12, which is a multiple of 3. So, all the numbers that can be made will be multiples of 3.

Zac's number must also be a multiple of 2, so it will be an even number.

That means his number must end in a 6.

So, there are two numbers that Zac could have made, 516 or 156.

b) We need to find a number that gives an answer of 153 with a remainder of 3, when it is divided by 4.

?

153	153	153	153	3

```
  1 5 3
×     4
-------
6 1 2
  2 1
```

612 + 3 = 615

Reena made the number 615.

Think together

1 Lexi rearranges these digit cards to make a 3-digit number.

When I divide my number by 5, the remainder is 1.

Lexi

What two numbers could Lexi have made?

Lexi could have made ⬜ and ⬜ .

2 a) What division calculation is shown here?

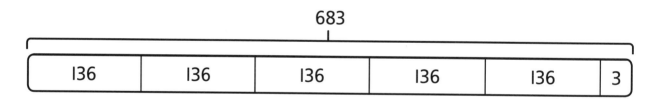

683

| 136 | 136 | 136 | 136 | 136 | 3 |

⬜ ÷ ⬜ = ⬜ r ⬜

b) When a 3-digit number is divided by 4, the answer is 47 r 1.

What is the number?

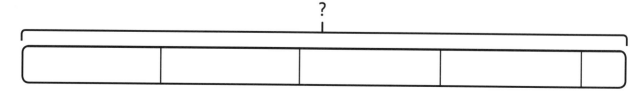

?

The number is ⬜ .

3 Richard has these digit cards.

| 0 | 1 | 2 | 3 | 4 | 5 | 7 | 9 |

I made a 3-digit number that I divided by one of the other digits.

My answer has a remainder of 4.

Richard

Write the division that Richard did.

Is there more than one possible division?

I think there are some numbers that you cannot divide by.

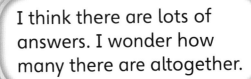

I think there are lots of answers. I wonder how many there are altogether.

51

End of unit check

1 What is the missing number in the bar model?

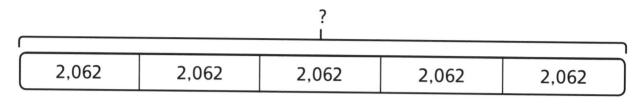

?

| 2,062 | 2,062 | 2,062 | 2,062 | 2,062 |

A 2,062   B 10,000   C 10,310   D 20,620

2 What multiplication is shown using the grid method?

600	80
60	8

A 34 × 22   B 20 × 36   C 68 × 68   D 24 × 32

3 What is the correct first step in the multiplication for 42 × 27?

A

```
      4 2
×     2 7
-------
  2 8 1 4
```

B

```
      4 2
×     2 7
-------
      8 4
```

C

```
      4 2
×     2 7
-------
  2 9 4
    1
```

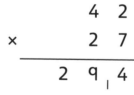

D

```
      4 2
×     2 7
-------
  1 6 8
    2
```

4 Which of these shows the correct answer to $3,892 \div 7$?

A
$$7 \overline{)\; 3 \;^48 \;^69 \;^62} \quad 0\;6\;9\;8\;r\,6$$

C
$$7 \overline{)\; 3 \;^38 \;^39 \;^42} \quad 0\;5\;5\;6$$

B
$$7 \overline{)\; 3 \;8 \;^19 \;^52} \quad 0\;1\;2\;7\;r\,3$$

D
$$7 \overline{)\; 3 \;8 \;9 \;2} \quad 0\;1\;1\;0$$

5 Max divides a 3-digit number by 5 and gets a remainder of 4. What number could Max have divided?

A 985 B 987 C 989 D 1,004

6 A small car holds 4 people.

How many cars would be needed to take 137 people?

A 34 B 35 C 36 D 141

7 Max has a large sack of apples.

If he put them into bags of 4 he would have 72 full bags and 3 apples left over.

If he puts 5 apples into each bag instead, how many bags will he fill? Will there be any apples left over?

53

→ Practice book 5B p39

Unit 8
Fractions ①

In this unit we will ...

⚡ Find and use equivalent fractions

⚡ Convert between improper fractions and mixed numbers

⚡ Compare and order fractions

⚡ Understand fractions as division

⚡ Use fractions to show remainders

Do you remember what this model is called? We will use it to represent mixed numbers and improper fractions. Can you tell which is which?

$\frac{1}{4}$	$\frac{1}{4}$	$\frac{1}{4}$	$\frac{1}{4}$	$\frac{1}{4}$	$\frac{1}{4}$

1				$\frac{1}{4}$	$\frac{1}{4}$

We will need some maths words. Do you know what they all mean? Can you identify and explain the ones you already recognise?

equivalent   numerator   denominator

whole   fraction   simplify   expand

division   improper   mixed number

convert   sequence   order

greater than (>)   less than (<)   equal to (=)

We will need to represent different fractions. What fractions are shown here?

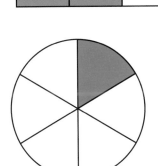

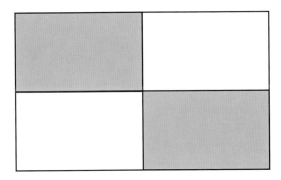

Equivalent fractions

Discover

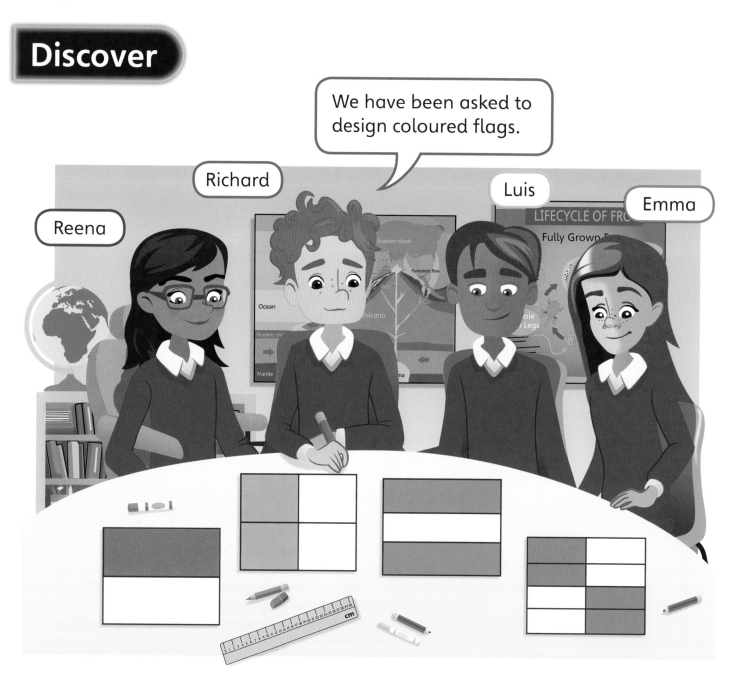

1 **a)** Which fractions are equivalent?

   b) Which fraction is the odd one out? Create two different fractions that are equivalent to the odd one out.

Share

a)

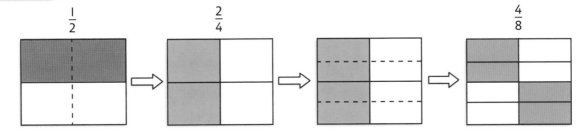

$\frac{1}{2}$ $\frac{2}{4}$ $\frac{4}{8}$

Multiply the numerators and denominators.

You can also divide to find equivalent fractions.

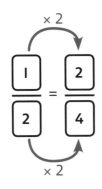

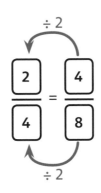

$\frac{1}{2} = \frac{2}{4} = \frac{4}{8}$

The equivalent fractions are $\frac{1}{2}$, $\frac{2}{4}$ and $\frac{4}{8}$.

b) The fraction shown on Luis's flag is the odd one out.

$\frac{2}{3}$ is not equivalent to the others.

I doubled the numerator and the denominator to find an equivalent fraction.

You do not always have to double to find equivalent fractions. I wonder how many other equivalent fractions I can find.

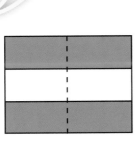

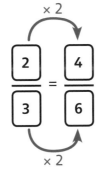

$\frac{2}{3} = \frac{4}{6}$

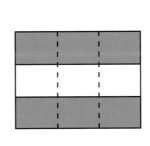

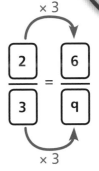

$\frac{2}{3} = \frac{6}{9}$

Two fractions equivalent to $\frac{2}{3}$ are $\frac{4}{6}$ and $\frac{6}{9}$.

Think together

1 a) Complete the equivalent fractions for these flags.

$$\frac{1}{3} = \frac{\boxed{}}{6}$$

b)

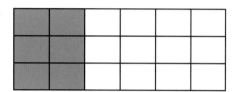
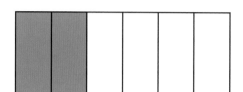

$$\frac{6}{18} = \frac{\boxed{}}{\boxed{}}$$

c) Design flags showing fractions equivalent to $\frac{4}{5}$.

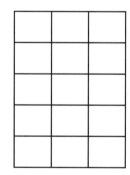

$$\frac{4}{5} = \frac{\boxed{}}{\boxed{}}$$

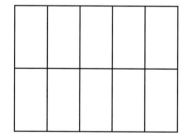

$$\frac{4}{5} = \frac{\boxed{}}{\boxed{}}$$

2 Find the missing numbers to complete these equivalent fractions.

Draw diagrams to show they are equivalent.

a) $\frac{4}{12} = \frac{2}{\boxed{}}$

b) $\frac{2}{\boxed{}} = \frac{10}{25}$

c) $\frac{2}{\boxed{}} = \frac{\boxed{}}{5}$

58

CHALLENGE

3 Reena is studying this pair of equivalent fractions.

She discovers the following relationship.

$$\div 3 \left(\frac{5}{15} = \frac{10}{30} \right) \div 3$$

Max then created this fraction pair.

$$\times 3 \left(\frac{3}{9} = \frac{12}{36} \right) \times 3$$

Reena says, 'I think all four fractions might be equivalent.'

Do you agree?

I will try to convert these fractions into simpler fractions.

Remember that **simplifying** a fraction means finding an equivalent fraction with a smaller numerator and denominator.

59

→ **Practice book 5B p42**

Converting improper fractions to mixed numbers

Discover

I'm painting Lee's room blue.

$\frac{1}{2}$ l $\frac{1}{2}$ l $\frac{1}{2}$ l $\frac{1}{2}$ l $\frac{1}{2}$ l

Sofia

1 **a)** Each can holds $\frac{1}{2}$ litre of paint. How much paint does Sofia have in total?

b) Sofia buys another $\frac{1}{2}$ l can of paint. How much paint does she have now?

Share

a)

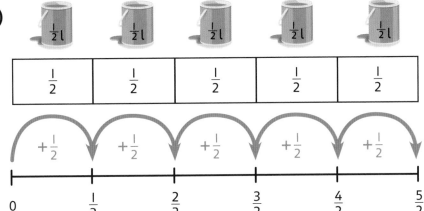

There are 5 half litres of paint.

5 halves is $\frac{5}{2}$. Sofia has $\frac{5}{2}$ litres of paint.

Two half litres make one whole litre.

$\frac{2}{2}$ is equivalent to 1.

$\frac{5}{2}$ is an **improper fraction**. The numerator is larger than the denominator.

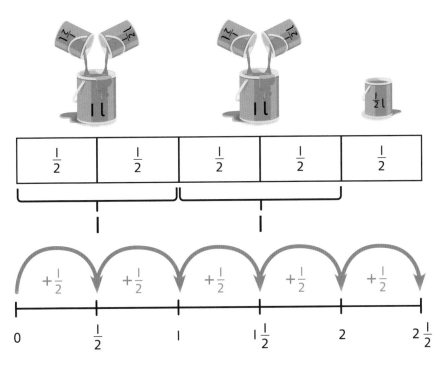

$\frac{1}{2} + \frac{1}{2} + \frac{1}{2} + \frac{1}{2} + \frac{1}{2}$

$1 \quad + \quad 1 \quad + \frac{1}{2}$

$\frac{5}{2} = 2\frac{1}{2}$

Sofia has $2\frac{1}{2}$ litres of paint.

b) Sofia has 6 half litres of paint.

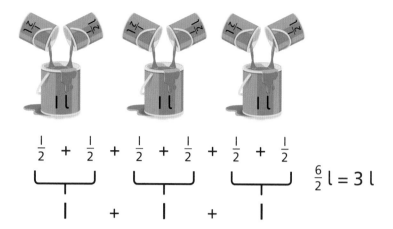

$\frac{1}{2}$ + $\frac{1}{2}$ + $\frac{1}{2}$ + $\frac{1}{2}$ + $\frac{1}{2}$ + $\frac{1}{2}$

$\frac{6}{2}$ l = 3 l

Sofia has 3 litres of paint now.

Think together

1 The hallway will be painted green. Green paint comes in cans of $\frac{1}{3}$ litre.

Sofia uses 10 cans. How much green paint does she use in total?

| $\frac{1}{3}$ | $\frac{1}{3}$ | $\frac{1}{3}$ | $\frac{1}{3}$ | $\frac{1}{3}$ | $\frac{1}{3}$ | $\frac{1}{3}$ | $\frac{1}{3}$ | $\frac{1}{3}$ | $\frac{1}{3}$ |

$\frac{10}{3}$ = $\boxed{}$ $\frac{\boxed{}}{3}$

Sofia uses $\boxed{}$ $\frac{\boxed{}}{\boxed{}}$ litres of green paint in total.

2 Convert these improper fractions into mixed numbers.

a) $\frac{5}{4}$ = ⬜ $\frac{⬜}{⬜}$ b) $\frac{13}{4}$ = ⬜ $\frac{⬜}{⬜}$ c) $\frac{15}{4}$ = ⬜ $\frac{⬜}{⬜}$ d) $\frac{41}{4}$ = ⬜ $\frac{⬜}{⬜}$

3 Complete each set. What stays the same and what changes? Explain the patterns of answers.

a) $\frac{17}{6}$ = ⬜ $\frac{⬜}{⬜}$ b) $\frac{24}{4}$ = ⬜ $\frac{⬜}{⬜}$

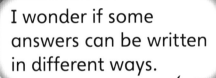

I wonder if some answers can be written in different ways.

$\frac{18}{6}$ = ⬜ $\frac{⬜}{⬜}$ $\frac{24}{5}$ = ⬜ $\frac{⬜}{⬜}$

$\frac{19}{6}$ = ⬜ $\frac{⬜}{⬜}$ $\frac{24}{6}$ = ⬜ $\frac{⬜}{⬜}$

$\frac{20}{6}$ = ⬜ $\frac{⬜}{⬜}$ $\frac{24}{7}$ = ⬜ $\frac{⬜}{⬜}$

$\frac{21}{6}$ = ⬜ $\frac{⬜}{⬜}$ $\frac{24}{8}$ = ⬜ $\frac{⬜}{⬜}$

I think I can simplify some of the fractions.

$\frac{22}{6}$ = ⬜ $\frac{⬜}{⬜}$ $\frac{24}{9}$ = ⬜ $\frac{⬜}{⬜}$

$\frac{23}{6}$ = ⬜ $\frac{⬜}{⬜}$ $\frac{24}{10}$ = ⬜ $\frac{⬜}{⬜}$

➜ **Practice book 5B p45**

Converting mixed numbers to improper fractions

Discover

Every child should receive $\frac{1}{4}$ of a fruit tart.

1 **a)** How many children can have $\frac{1}{4}$ of a fruit tart?

b) How many children could have $\frac{1}{8}$ of a fruit tart?

Share

a) There are 4 whole fruit tarts and one quarter of a fruit tart.

Each whole fruit tart splits into 4 quarters.

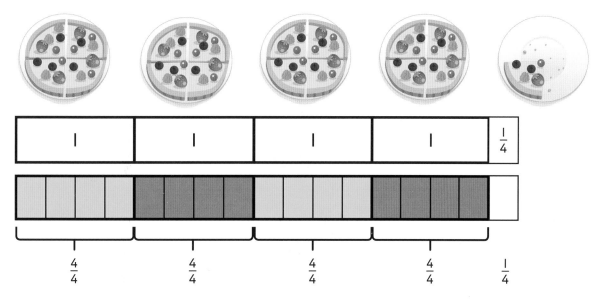

$$4 + 4 + 4 + 4 + 1 = 17$$

$$4\frac{1}{4} = \frac{17}{4}$$

There are 17 quarters. 17 children can each have a quarter of a fruit tart.

b) Each whole fruit tart splits into 8 eighths.

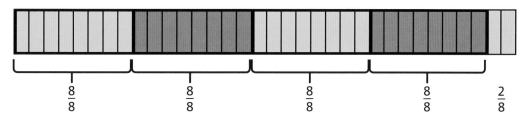

$$8 + 8 + 8 + 8 + 2 = 34$$

34 children could each have an eighth of a fruit tart.

I did this a different way. I knew that each $\frac{1}{4}$ split into 2 eighths, so I doubled 17.

65

Think together

1 At the picnic there are $3\frac{4}{5}$ pies. Each child is given $\frac{1}{5}$ of a pie.

How many children can each have $\frac{1}{5}$ of a pie?

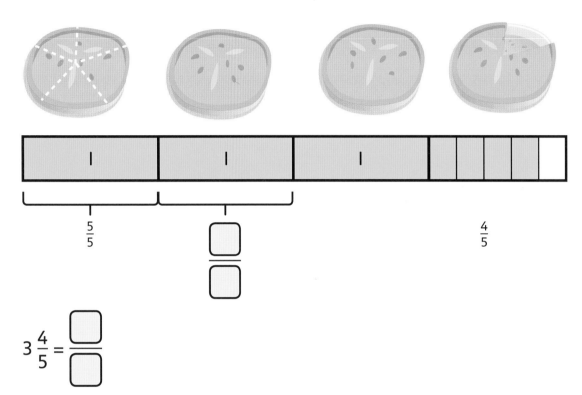

$\frac{5}{5}$ $\frac{\boxed{}}{\boxed{}}$ $\frac{4}{5}$

$3\frac{4}{5} = \dfrac{\boxed{}}{\boxed{}}$

$\boxed{}$ children can each have $\frac{1}{5}$ of a pie.

2 Write each mixed number as an improper fraction.

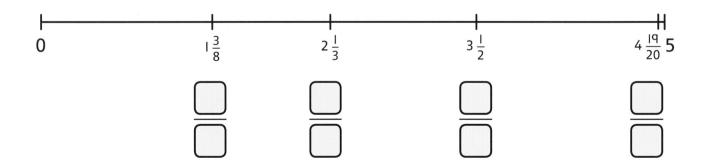

3 Bella is finding solutions to:

$$\bigstar \frac{1}{5} = \frac{\triangle}{5}$$

She chooses different numbers for ⭐ and looks at the effect on ▲ .

Complete the table and explain what happens to ▲ when you increase ⭐ by 1.

⭐	▲
1	☐
2	☐
3	☐
4	☐
5	☐
10	☐

67

→ **Practice book 5B p48**

Number sequences

Discover

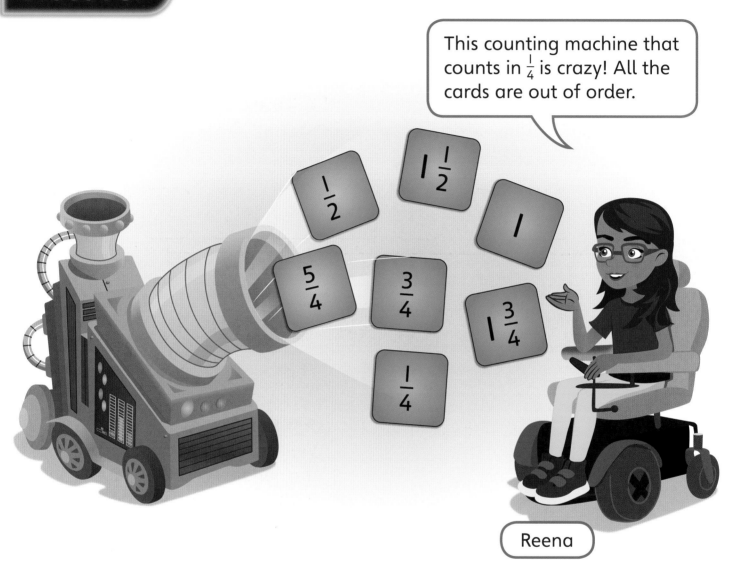

This counting machine that counts in $\frac{1}{4}$ is crazy! All the cards are out of order.

Reena

1 **a)** Order the cards to make a counting sequence.

b) How many cards will the machine print in total until it reaches $5\frac{1}{2}$?

Share

a) The machine counts in quarters.

The cards include improper fractions and mixed numbers, and some of the fractions have been simplified.

I will use a number line to organise the cards.

I will use diagrams to help me order the numbers.

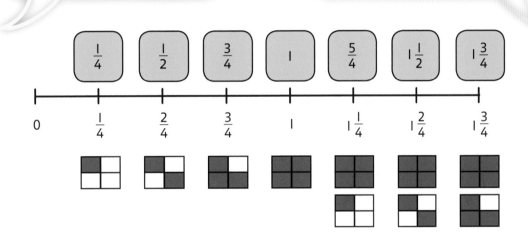

b) Every card increases the count by $\frac{1}{4}$.

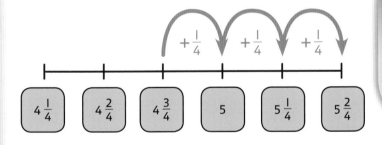

I know that a fraction with the denominator 2 can be written as an equivalent fraction with the denominator 4, because 4 is a multiple of 2.

There are 22 quarters in $5\frac{2}{4}$.

$5\frac{1}{2} = 5\frac{2}{4}$

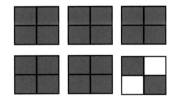

The machine will print 22 cards in total until it reaches $5\frac{1}{2}$.

Think together

1 Another machine counts in intervals of $\frac{1}{3}$.

Put the cards in order and work out the missing numbers.

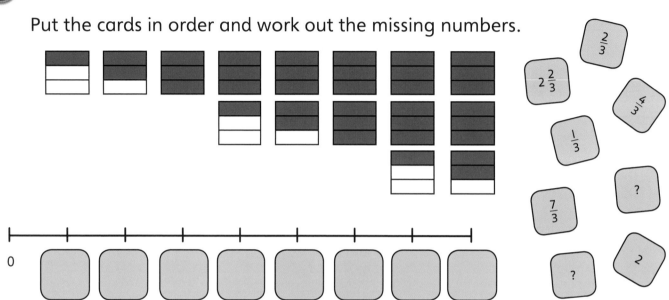

2 Complete and continue each sequence.

a)

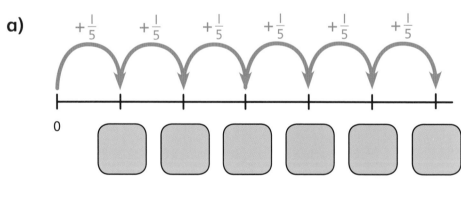

b)

| 4 | $3\frac{3}{4}$ | $3\frac{1}{2}$ | $3\frac{1}{4}$ | | | |

c)

$1\frac{5}{6}$ 2 $2\frac{1}{6}$

3 Work out the rule of each sequence and find the missing numbers.

a)

4 ☐ ☐ ☐ ☐ 5

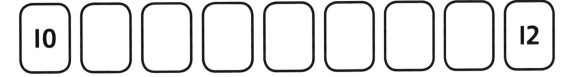

The first sequence has 4 blanks, so I think it must count in quarters.

There are four gaps, but I think you need to count 5 times from the start to the finish.

b)

| 10 | ☐ | ☐ | ☐ | ☐ | ☐ | ☐ | ☐ | 12 |

c)

| $7\frac{1}{2}$ | ☐ | ☐ | ☐ | ☐ | ☐ | ☐ | ☐ | ☐ | 6 |

→ Practice book 5B p51

Comparing and ordering fractions ❶

Discover

The school library conducts a survey before ordering new books to see what type of books children like. The poster shows the results.

Type of book	Science fiction	Non-fiction	Mystery fiction	Comic
Fraction of children who like this type	$\frac{5}{8}$	$\frac{3}{5}$	$\frac{3}{8}$	$\frac{3}{4}$

Amelia   Jamie   Ebo   Reena   Aki

❶ a) Do more children like science fiction or mystery fiction?
Do more children like science fiction or comic books?

b) Do more children like non-fiction or mystery fiction?

Share

a)

Science fiction $\frac{5}{8}$

Mystery fiction $\frac{3}{8}$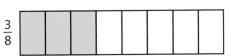

More children like science fiction than mystery fiction.

5 equal parts are greater than 3 equal parts.

This is easy to compare because the denominators are the same.

Science fiction $\frac{5}{8}$

Comic books $\frac{3}{4}$

$\frac{6}{8} > \frac{5}{8}$, so $\frac{3}{4} > \frac{5}{8}$.

More children like comic books than science fiction.

The denominators are not the same. I will use equivalent fractions so I can compare more easily: $\frac{3}{4} = \frac{6}{8}$.

b) Each fraction has the same number of parts, but the parts are different sizes.

Non-fiction $\frac{3}{5}$

Mystery fiction $\frac{3}{8}$

3 larger parts are greater than 3 smaller parts.

$\frac{3}{5} > \frac{3}{8}$

More children like non-fiction than like mystery fiction.

Think together

1 Amelia and Mo are reading the same book in class.

Amelia has read $\frac{4}{5}$, Mo has read $\frac{11}{15}$. Who has read more?

Amelia

Mo

$\frac{4}{5}$ ◯ $\frac{11}{15}$

_____ has read more.

2 Put these cards in order from smallest to largest.

| $\frac{2}{6}$ | $\frac{2}{3}$ | $\frac{5}{12}$ | $\frac{5}{6}$ | $\frac{3}{6}$ | $\frac{1}{6}$ |

☐/☐ , ☐/☐ , ☐/☐ , ☐/☐ , ☐/☐ , ☐/☐

First I will sort them into fractions which are greater than and less than a half.

3 **a)** Max is trying to find all the possible missing numbers.

$$\frac{5}{9} > \frac{\square}{18}$$

$$\frac{\square}{6} < \frac{12}{18}$$

Max says, 'I think one of these has more solutions than the other.'

Do you agree? Explain your answer.

b) Explain how to find more than one solution to these problems.

$$\frac{3}{5} < \frac{\square}{\square} < \frac{4}{5}$$

$$1 > \frac{\square}{\square} > \frac{3}{4}$$

75

→ Practice book 5B p54

Comparing and ordering fractions ❷

Discover

café $3\frac{1}{4}$ miles

shop $2\frac{3}{4}$ miles

beach $2\frac{1}{3}$ miles

castle $2\frac{1}{2}$ miles

garage $3\frac{1}{2}$ miles

pier $\frac{13}{4}$ miles

I a) Which is closer, the café or the shop? Is the beach or the castle closer?

b) Which is farther away, the garage or the pier?

Share

a) When comparing mixed numbers, first compare the whole number parts.

> The café is more than 3 miles away. The shop is less than 3 miles away.

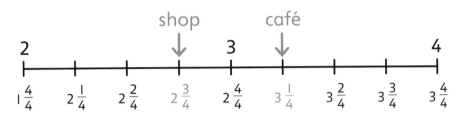

shop   café

2   3   4

$1\frac{4}{4}$ $2\frac{1}{4}$ $2\frac{2}{4}$ $2\frac{3}{4}$ $2\frac{4}{4}$ $3\frac{1}{4}$ $3\frac{2}{4}$ $3\frac{3}{4}$ $3\frac{4}{4}$

$3 > 2$, so $3\frac{1}{4}$ miles $> 2\frac{3}{4}$ miles. The shop is closer than the café.

If the whole number parts are equal, compare the fraction parts.

Beach: $2\frac{1}{3}$ miles

Castle: $2\frac{1}{2}$ miles

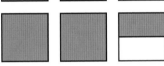

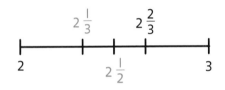

$2\frac{1}{3}$ $2\frac{2}{3}$

2          $2\frac{1}{2}$ 3

$\frac{1}{3} < \frac{1}{2}$, so $2\frac{1}{3}$ miles $< 2\frac{1}{2}$ miles.

The beach is closer than the castle.

b) To compare, convert both of the distances into improper fractions or mixed numbers.

Garage:

$3\frac{1}{2}$ miles $= \frac{7}{2} = \frac{14}{4}$

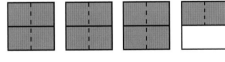

Pier:

$\frac{13}{4}$ miles $= 3\frac{1}{4}$

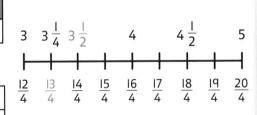

3   $3\frac{1}{4}$ $3\frac{1}{2}$ 4 $4\frac{1}{2}$ 5

$\frac{12}{4}$ $\frac{13}{4}$ $\frac{14}{4}$ $\frac{15}{4}$ $\frac{16}{4}$ $\frac{17}{4}$ $\frac{18}{4}$ $\frac{19}{4}$ $\frac{20}{4}$

The garage is farther away than the pier.

Think together

1 Who has walked farther?

I have walked $1\frac{3}{4}$ miles.

Amelia

I have walked $1\frac{1}{2}$ miles.

Max

$1\frac{3}{4}$ ◯ $1\frac{1}{2}$

I will use the diagrams to help me compare.

_____ has walked farther.

2 Who has more juice?

Each carton holds $\frac{1}{3}$ litre of juice. I have 16 cartons.

Jen

I have $5\frac{1}{2}$ litres of juice.

Toshi

$\frac{16}{3}$ ◯ $5\frac{1}{2}$

_____ has more juice.

3 Sacks A, B and C are filled with weights.

Each weight has a mass of $\frac{1}{16}$ kg.

How many weights could be in each sack?

CHALLENGE

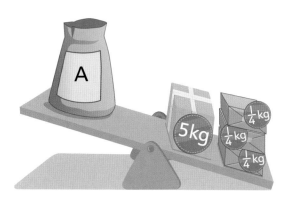

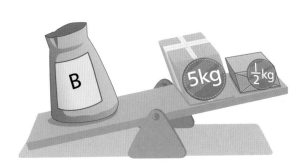

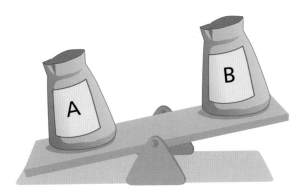

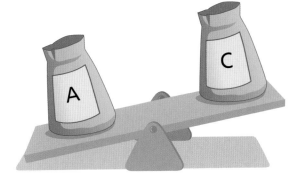

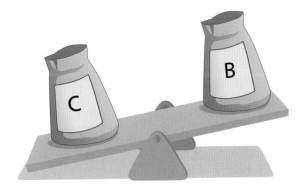

79

→ **Practice book 5B p57**

Fractions as division ①

Discover

① **a)** If 2 pizzas are shared equally between 3 people, how much pizza will each person get?

b) 2 pizzas are to be shared between 4 people. Show how this can be done in different ways.

Share

a) To work out 2 ÷ 3, share the pizzas one at a time.

Share the first pizza. Each person gets 1 third.

$$1 \div 3 = \tfrac{1}{3}$$

Share the second pizza. Each person gets another third.

 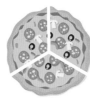    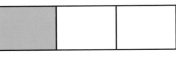

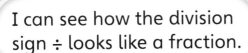

Each person gets $\tfrac{2}{3}$ of a pizza.

$$2 \div 3 = \tfrac{1}{3} + \tfrac{1}{3}$$

$$2 \div 3 = \tfrac{2}{3}$$

I can see how the division sign ÷ looks like a fraction.

b)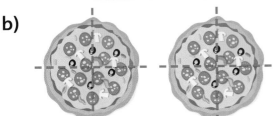

Each person gets $\tfrac{1}{4}$ of each pizza.

$$2 \div 4 = \tfrac{1}{4} + \tfrac{1}{4} = \tfrac{2}{4} = \tfrac{1}{2}$$

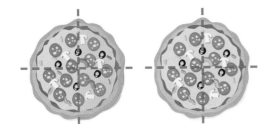

Each person gets $\tfrac{1}{2}$ of one pizza.

$$2 \div 4 = \tfrac{1}{2}$$

Think together

1 3 pizzas are divided equally among 5 people. How much does each person get?

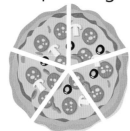 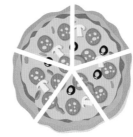 

$\frac{1}{5}$	$\frac{1}{5}$	$\frac{1}{5}$	$\frac{1}{5}$	$\frac{1}{5}$

$\frac{1}{5}$	$\frac{1}{5}$	$\frac{1}{5}$	$\frac{1}{5}$	$\frac{1}{5}$

$\frac{1}{5}$	$\frac{1}{5}$	$\frac{1}{5}$	$\frac{1}{5}$	$\frac{1}{5}$

$3 \div 5 = \frac{1}{5} + \frac{1}{5} + \frac{1}{5}$

This looks like $\frac{3}{15}$. But I do not think they each get $\frac{3}{15}$ of a pizza.

I need to work out what each bar represents.

Each person receives $\dfrac{\square}{\square}$ of a pizza.

2 7 artists share 4 kg of clay equally. How much clay does each artist have?

I kg   I kg   I kg   I kg

$\boxed{} \div \boxed{} = \dfrac{\square}{\square}$

$\frac{1}{7}$	$\frac{1}{7}$	$\frac{1}{7}$	$\frac{1}{7}$	$\frac{1}{7}$	$\frac{1}{7}$	$\frac{1}{7}$

Each artist has $\dfrac{\square}{\square}$ kg of clay.

3 **a)** Use the number cards to complete each statement.

You can only use a card once.

| 1 | 2 | 3 | 4 | 5 | 6 | 7 | 8 | 9 | 10 |

| 11 | 12 | 13 | 14 | 15 | 16 | 17 | 18 | 19 | 20 |

$\boxed{} \div \boxed{} = \dfrac{1}{6}$

$\boxed{} \div \boxed{} = \dfrac{2}{6}$

$\boxed{} \div \boxed{} = \dfrac{3}{6}$

$\boxed{} \div \boxed{} = \dfrac{4}{6}$

$\boxed{} \div \boxed{} = \dfrac{5}{6}$

I can think of many different solutions for $\dfrac{3}{6}$.

b) Which cards cannot be used in any of the statements? Explain why.

→ **Practice book 5B p60**

Fractions as division 2

Discover

Emma   Mo   Aki   Mrs Dean

1 a) Emma says, 'If you divide 11 by 4 you get a remainder.'

Complete the division and decide what to do with the remainder.

b) Mo says, 'Let's split every roll into 4 parts.'

Show how this solves the problem.

Share

a)

$11 \div 4 = 2$ remainder 3

Divide each remaining roll into 4 pieces.

Give each person $\frac{1}{4}$ of each remaining roll. Keep doing this until all of the remaining rolls have been shared out.

$11 \div 4 = 2\frac{3}{4}$

Now each person receives $2\frac{3}{4}$ rolls to eat.

b) Each roll is split into quarters. Each person receives $\frac{1}{4}$ of each roll.

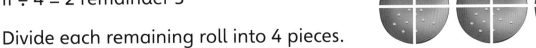

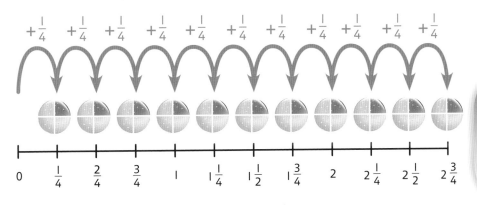

The fraction $\frac{11}{4}$ is another way of writing the division $11 \div 4$.

$11 \div 4 = \frac{1}{4} + \frac{1}{4} + \frac{1}{4} + \frac{1}{4} + \frac{1}{4} + \frac{1}{4} + \frac{1}{4} + \frac{1}{4} + \frac{1}{4} + \frac{1}{4} + \frac{1}{4} = \frac{11}{4}$

Each person receives $\frac{11}{4}$. This is equivalent to $2\frac{3}{4}$.

Think together

1 Mrs Dean, Emma, Mo and Aki have 5 litres of water to share equally between them.

How much water can each person have?

$5 ÷ 4 = \boxed{}$ remainder $\boxed{}$

$5 ÷ 4 = \dfrac{\boxed{}}{\boxed{}}$

$5 ÷ 4 = \boxed{}\dfrac{\boxed{}}{\boxed{}}$

2 a) Mrs Dean, Emma, Mo and Aki plan to walk 10 miles in the first 3 hours. How far will they need to walk in each hour?

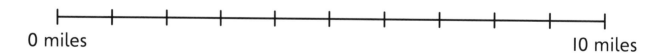

0 miles   10 miles

b) In the afternoon they plan to walk 11 miles in 3 hours. How many miles per hour is this?

I wonder if I can use my answer to the first part to help.

CHALLENGE

3 Andy has solved a division.

$$\begin{array}{r} 0\ 3\ 3\ \text{r}\ 1 \\ 3\overline{)1\ ^10\ ^10} \end{array}$$

$100 \div 3 = 33$ remainder 1

He says, 'I will write the remainder as a fraction. I think the answer is either $33\frac{1}{100}$ or $33\frac{1}{3}$.'

a) Explain which answer is correct, using a diagram to show your reasoning.

I wonder what problem this division might solve. I will think of a story problem to see if that helps.

b) Complete these divisions, writing any remainders as a fraction.

$100 \div 6$	$22 \div 6$
$100 \div 7$	$22 \div 7$
$100 \div 8$	$22 \div 8$

I will write the division as an improper fraction.

87

End of unit check

1 Which representation is not equivalent to $\frac{10}{15}$?

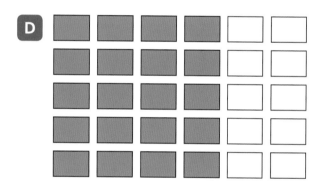

2 Convert $\frac{14}{8}$ into a mixed number.

A $1\frac{4}{8}$ B $14\frac{1}{8}$ C $8\frac{1}{4}$ D $1\frac{3}{4}$

3 Which fraction is less than $\frac{15}{20}$?

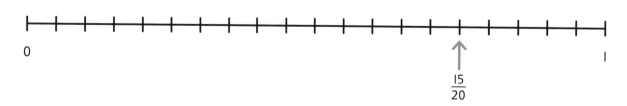

A $\frac{4}{5}$ B $\frac{7}{10}$ C $\frac{17}{20}$ D $\frac{3}{4}$

4 Which sequence increases in steps of $\frac{1}{6}$?

A $\boxed{2\frac{1}{6}}$ $\boxed{2\frac{1}{3}}$ $\boxed{2\frac{1}{2}}$ $\boxed{\frac{8}{3}}$

B
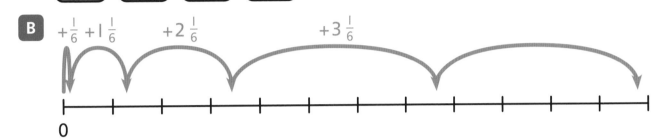

C $\boxed{\frac{12}{6}}$ $\boxed{\frac{11}{6}}$ $\boxed{\frac{10}{6}}$ $\boxed{\frac{9}{6}}$ $\boxed{\frac{8}{6}}$

D $\frac{1}{6}, \frac{7}{6}, \frac{13}{6}, \frac{19}{6}, \frac{25}{6}$

5 Which division is incorrect?

A $10 \div 3 = 3\frac{1}{3}$ **B** $3 \div 6 = \frac{1}{2}$ **C** $6 \div 7 = 1\frac{1}{6}$ **D** $7 \div 6 = 1\frac{1}{6}$

6 Order these cards from smallest to largest.

$\boxed{1\frac{12}{20}}$ $\boxed{\frac{8}{5}}$ $\boxed{\frac{5}{4}}$ $\boxed{1\frac{3}{10}}$ $\boxed{1\frac{12}{15}}$

89

→ **Practice book 5B p66**

Unit 9
Fractions ②

In this unit we will ...

⚡ Add and subtract fractions with the same denominator

⚡ Add and subtract fractions, including mixed numbers, where one denominator is a multiple of the other

⚡ Solve word problems involving fractions

How can you add these two fractions?

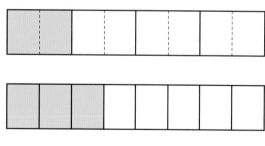

$$\frac{1}{4} + \frac{3}{8}$$

We will need some maths words.
Do you know what they all mean?

add   subtract   proper fraction

improper fraction   convert   simplify

equivalent fraction   mixed number

denominator   numerator

whole   efficient   common denominator

We need to be able to convert between mixed numbers and improper fractions. Use your skills to convert $2\frac{1}{3}$ into an improper fraction.

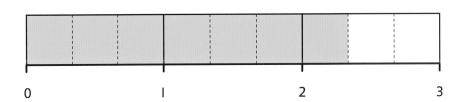

0   1   2   3

Adding and subtracting fractions with the same denominator

Discover

Lexi

1 **a)** Lexi chooses two cards.

Her cards add to $1\frac{3}{8}$.

Which two cards could Lexi have chosen?

b) Lexi chooses two different cards.

The two cards have a sum of 1 and their difference is $\frac{1}{4}$.

Which two cards did Lexi choose?

Share

a) Change $1\frac{3}{8}$ to an improper fraction.

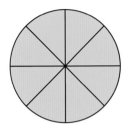

$$1\frac{3}{8} = \frac{11}{8}$$

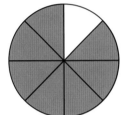 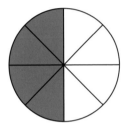

$$\frac{7}{8} + \frac{4}{8} = \frac{11}{8}$$

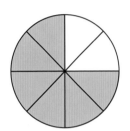

$$\frac{6}{8} + \frac{5}{8} = \frac{11}{8}$$

Lexi could have chosen $\frac{7}{8}$ and $\frac{4}{8}$, or $\frac{6}{8}$ and $\frac{5}{8}$.

b) The cards have a sum of 1.

The cards have a difference of $\frac{1}{4}$.

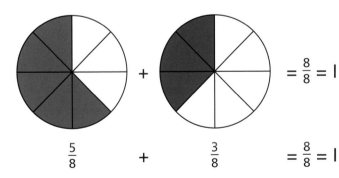

$$= \frac{8}{8} = 1$$

$$\frac{5}{8} \quad + \quad \frac{3}{8} \quad = \frac{8}{8} = 1$$

$$\times 2$$
$$\frac{1}{4} = \frac{2}{8}$$
$$\times 2$$

$$\frac{5}{8} - \frac{3}{8} = \frac{2}{8} = \frac{1}{4}$$

The fraction cards Lexi chose were $\frac{5}{8}$ and $\frac{3}{8}$.

I remember that I can also write 1 as $\frac{8}{8}$.

93

Think together

1 Lexi is working out the answers to some questions.

Help Lexi complete her work.

a) Which two cards have a sum of $\frac{5}{8}$?

$$\frac{3}{8} + \frac{\square}{\square} = \frac{5}{8}$$

b) Which two cards have a difference of $\frac{6}{8}$?

$$\frac{\square}{\square} - \frac{\square}{\square} = \frac{6}{8}$$

c) Which three cards have a sum of $\frac{15}{8}$?

$$\frac{\square}{\square} + \frac{\square}{\square} + \frac{\square}{\square} = \frac{15}{8}$$

d) Which three cards have a sum of $1\frac{5}{8}$?

$$\frac{\square}{\square} + \frac{\square}{\square} + \frac{\square}{\square} = 1\frac{5}{8}$$

2 Danny has some different fraction cards.

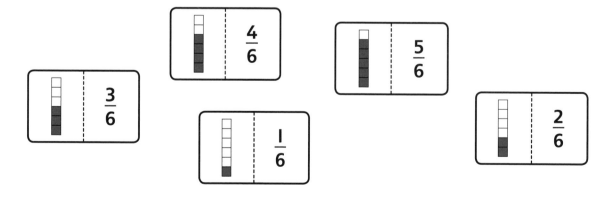

Which two cards have a sum of 1 and have a difference of $\frac{2}{6}$?

3 **a)** Danny and Lexi pick these four fractions.

$$\frac{4}{6} \qquad \frac{1}{8} \qquad \frac{7}{8} \qquad \frac{2}{6}$$

What is the sum of all of the fractions?

> I am not sure if you can add fractions if they do not have the same denominator.

> You do not have to add them all at once!

b) Lexi and Danny each choose two different cards from their own pile.

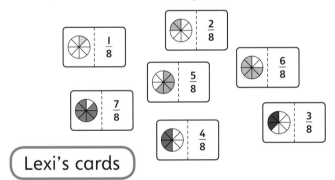

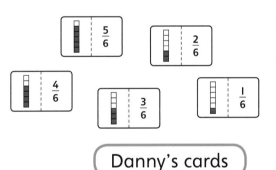

Lexi's cards

Danny's cards

'The sum of my two cards is $1\frac{1}{2}$,' says Lexi.

'That is the same as the sum of my two cards!' replies Danny.

What two cards could Lexi and Danny have chosen?

1						1					
$\frac{1}{2}$			$\frac{1}{2}$			$\frac{1}{2}$			$\frac{1}{2}$		
$\frac{1}{6}$	$\frac{1}{6}$	$\frac{1}{6}$	$\frac{1}{6}$	$\frac{1}{6}$	$\frac{1}{6}$	$\frac{1}{6}$	$\frac{1}{6}$	$\frac{1}{6}$	$\frac{1}{6}$	$\frac{1}{6}$	$\frac{1}{6}$
$\frac{1}{8}$	$\frac{1}{8}$	$\frac{1}{8}$	$\frac{1}{8}$	$\frac{1}{8}$	$\frac{1}{8}$	$\frac{1}{8}$	$\frac{1}{8}$	$\frac{1}{8}$	$\frac{1}{8}$	$\frac{1}{8}$	$\frac{1}{8}$

→ Practice book 5B p68

Adding and subtracting fractions ❶

Discover

There is $\frac{2}{5}$ of a litre of juice in the jug.

❶ **a)** How much pizza is left in total?

b) There is $\frac{2}{5}$ of a litre of juice. Danny drinks $\frac{3}{10}$ of a litre.

How much juice is left in the jug?

Share

a) 1 out of 3 slices of the first pizza is left. $\frac{1}{3}$ is left.

1 out of 6 slices of the second pizza is left. $\frac{1}{6}$ is left.

A common denominator of these fractions is 6.

$\frac{1}{3}$ is equivalent to $\frac{2}{6}$.

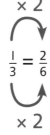

$\times 2$

$\frac{1}{3} = \frac{2}{6}$

$\times 2$

> To add or subtract fractions, the denominators need to be the same. This is called a **common denominator**.

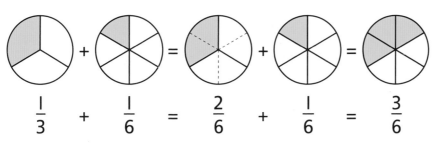

$$\frac{1}{3} \quad + \quad \frac{1}{6} \quad = \quad \frac{2}{6} \quad + \quad \frac{1}{6} \quad = \quad \frac{3}{6}$$

$\frac{3}{6}$ can be simplified to $\frac{1}{2}$. There is $\frac{1}{2}$ of a pizza left in total.

b) Start with $\frac{2}{5}$ and subtract $\frac{3}{10}$.

A common denominator is 10.

$\frac{2}{5}$ is equivalent to $\frac{4}{10}$.

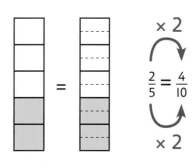

$\times 2$

$\frac{2}{5} = \frac{4}{10}$

$\times 2$

$$\frac{2}{5} - \frac{3}{10} = \frac{4}{10} - \frac{3}{10} = \frac{1}{10}$$

There is $\frac{1}{10}$ of a litre of juice left.

$\leftarrow \frac{1}{10}$

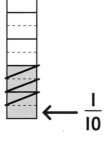

97

Think together

1 At the start of the party there were two cakes. Here is what is left.

How much cake is left in total?

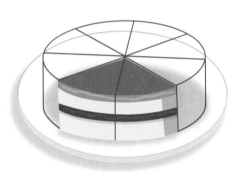

$$\frac{1}{4} = \frac{\boxed{}}{8}$$

$$\frac{1}{4} + \frac{3}{8} = \frac{\boxed{}}{8} + \frac{3}{8} = \frac{\boxed{}}{8}$$

There is $\frac{\boxed{}}{8}$ cake left in total.

2 Use the fraction strips to work out $\frac{2}{3} + \frac{1}{9}$.

$$\frac{2}{3} = \frac{\boxed{}}{9}$$

$$\frac{2}{3} + \frac{1}{9} = \frac{\boxed{}}{9} + \frac{\boxed{}}{9} = \frac{\boxed{}}{9}$$

3 **a)** Use the diagrams to work out $\frac{1}{8} + \frac{3}{4}$.

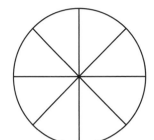 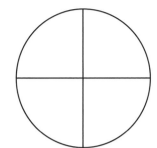

Write your answer, then explain your method to a friend.

$$\frac{1}{8} + \frac{3}{4} = \frac{\Box}{\Box}$$

b) Use your own diagrams to solve these calculations:

$$\frac{7}{8} - \frac{1}{2} = \frac{\Box}{\Box}$$

$$\frac{4}{15} + \frac{1}{5} = \frac{\Box}{\Box}$$

$$\frac{5}{6} - \frac{7}{12} = \frac{\Box}{\Box} = \frac{\Box}{\Box}$$

First I will find a common denominator. Then I will use my knowledge of equivalent fractions.

I will cross out the parts on my diagram as I subtract, to help me keep track.

99

Adding and subtracting fractions ❷

Discover

It took me 10 minutes to run the first $\frac{3}{8}$ of the course.

I ran the next $\frac{1}{4}$ in 5 minutes.

Bella

1 **a)** What fraction of the course has Bella run so far?

b) Max ran the first $\frac{1}{3}$ of the course in 10 minutes.

He ran the next $\frac{1}{6}$ of the course in 8 minutes.

He ran the next $\frac{5}{12}$ of the course in 5 minutes.

What fraction of the course has he completed in total?

Share

a) Bella ran $\frac{3}{8}$ of the course and then another $\frac{1}{4}$.

Find the common denominator and change $\frac{1}{4}$ to an equivalent fraction.

> I found 8 as a common denominator as it is a multiple of 4 and 8.

$\times 2$

$\frac{1}{4} = \frac{2}{8}$

$\times 2$

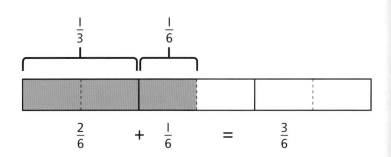

$\frac{3}{8} \quad + \quad \frac{1}{4} \qquad = \qquad \frac{3}{8} \quad + \quad \frac{2}{8} \quad = \quad \frac{5}{8}$

Bella has run $\frac{5}{8}$ of the course so far.

b) Method I

First add $\frac{1}{3}$ and $\frac{1}{6}$.

$\times 2$

$\frac{1}{3} = \frac{2}{6}$ So $\frac{1}{3} + \frac{1}{6} = \frac{2}{6} + \frac{1}{6} = \frac{3}{6}$

$\times 2$

$\frac{1}{3} \qquad \frac{1}{6}$

$\frac{2}{6} \qquad + \qquad \frac{1}{6} \qquad = \qquad \frac{3}{6}$

Now add $\frac{5}{12}$.

$\frac{3}{6} = \frac{6}{12}$

So $\frac{3}{6} + \frac{5}{12} = \frac{6}{12} + \frac{5}{12} = \frac{11}{12}$

$\frac{3}{6} \qquad \frac{5}{12}$

$\frac{6}{12} \qquad + \qquad \frac{5}{12} \qquad = \qquad \frac{11}{12}$

Method 2

$\frac{1}{3} \qquad \frac{1}{6} \qquad \frac{5}{12}$

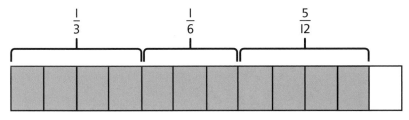

$\frac{1}{3} + \frac{1}{6} + \frac{5}{12} = \frac{4}{12} + \frac{2}{12} + \frac{5}{12} = \frac{11}{12}$

Max has run $\frac{11}{12}$ of the course in total.

> I think I can add all three fractions together in one go. I know a common denominator is 12 as this is a multiple of 3, 6 and 12.

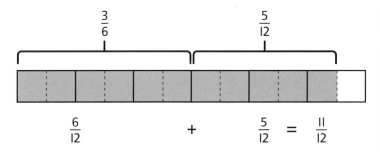

Think together

1 Luis ran $\frac{3}{5}$ km. Danny ran $\frac{9}{10}$ km.

How much further did Danny run?

$\frac{3}{5}$ is equivalent to $\frac{\boxed{}}{10}$

Luis

Danny

Danny ran $\frac{\boxed{}}{\boxed{}}$ km further than Luis.

2 Lexi times how long it takes her to complete three obstacles.

- It takes her $\frac{1}{6}$ of a minute to climb a wall.

- It takes her $\frac{1}{4}$ of a minute to run across a muddy track.

- It takes her $\frac{7}{12}$ of a minute to do the zipwire.

How long does it take Lexi to complete all three obstacles?

It takes Lexi _____ to complete the three obstacles.

CHALLENGE

3 Max, Alex and Zac are a team in a relay race.

They each run a different distance.

- Max runs $\frac{5}{12}$ of the distance.

- Alex runs $\frac{7}{24}$ of the distance.

- Zac runs the remaining distance.

a) What fraction of the race does Zac complete?

b) Who runs the furthest?

I am going to find a common denominator first. I wonder if I could use 24.

I can find the total run by Max and Alex. That will help me work out how far Zac has run.

103

Adding fractions ❶

Discover

❶ a) What fraction of an hour did Reena spend on her maths homework?

b) How much time did Reena spend in total on her maths and English homework? Write your answer as a fraction.

Share

a)

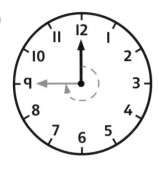 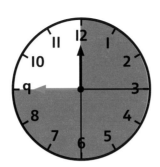

I drew a clock and showed that 45 minutes is equal to $\frac{3}{4}$ of an hour.

45 minutes is $\frac{3}{4}$ of an hour.

Reena spent $\frac{3}{4}$ of an hour on her maths homework.

b) Reena spent $\frac{5}{12}$ of an hour on her English homework.

The total time is $\frac{3}{4} + \frac{5}{12}$.

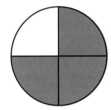 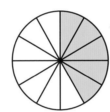

Maths: $\frac{3}{4}$ of an hour   English: $\frac{5}{12}$ of an hour

A common denominator is 12.

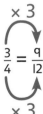

$$\frac{3}{4} = \frac{9}{12}$$

× 3

First I found a common denominator. Then I added the fractions to find the total.

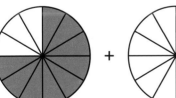 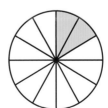

$$\frac{9}{12} + \frac{5}{12} = \frac{14}{12} = 1\frac{2}{12} = 1\frac{1}{6}$$

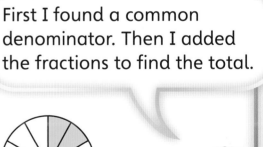

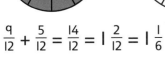

Think together

1 Reena spent $\frac{2}{3}$ of an hour watching TV.

She spent $\frac{5}{6}$ of an hour on the computer.

What is the total amount of time Reena spent watching TV and on the computer?

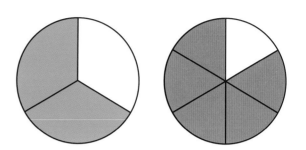

$$\frac{2}{3} = \frac{\boxed{}}{6}$$

$$\frac{\boxed{}}{6} + \frac{5}{6} = \frac{\boxed{}}{6}$$

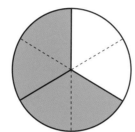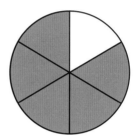

$$= \boxed{}\frac{\boxed{}}{6}$$

$$= \boxed{}\frac{\boxed{}}{2}$$

Reena spent $\boxed{}\dfrac{\boxed{}}{\boxed{}}$ hours in total watching TV and on the computer.

2 Amelia drinks $\frac{4}{5}$ of a glass of water.

Later she drinks $\frac{9}{10}$ of another glass of water.

How many glasses of water does she drink in total?

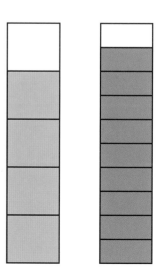

3 **a)** Use the fraction wall to help you add the following fractions.

$\frac{1}{2}$		$\frac{1}{2}$	

Fraction wall with rows: $\frac{1}{2}$, $\frac{1}{3}$, $\frac{1}{4}$, $\frac{1}{5}$, $\frac{1}{6}$, $\frac{1}{8}$, $\frac{1}{9}$, $\frac{1}{10}$, $\frac{1}{12}$

$$\frac{3}{5} + \frac{7}{10} \qquad \frac{1}{2} + \frac{11}{12} \qquad \frac{7}{9} + \frac{1}{3} \qquad \frac{3}{4} + \frac{5}{8}$$

b) Work out the missing fractions.

$$\frac{3}{4} + \frac{7}{20} = \boxed{}\, \frac{\boxed{}}{\boxed{}} \qquad\qquad \frac{11}{18} + \frac{4}{9} = \boxed{}\, \frac{\boxed{}}{\boxed{}}$$

$$\frac{4}{5} + \frac{\boxed{}}{\boxed{}} = 1\frac{4}{15} \qquad\qquad \frac{4}{7} + \frac{\boxed{}}{\boxed{}} = 1\frac{2}{21}$$

Where there is a mixed number, I will start by converting it to an improper fraction. I think this will help me.

I am going to change each fraction to have the same denominator and see if this helps.

107

Adding fractions ❷

Discover

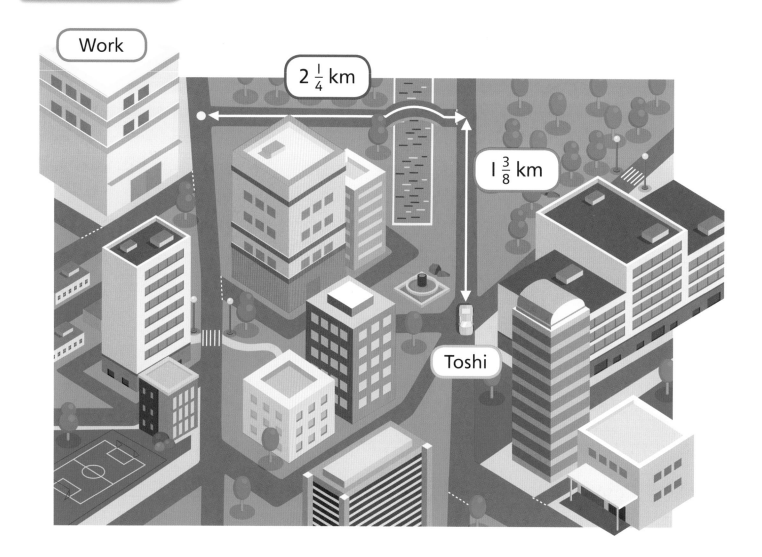

I a) Toshi leaves work and drives along two roads in the city.

How far has Toshi driven so far?

b) Toshi turns left and drives along another street to his home.

He has now driven $4\frac{1}{8}$ km in total.

How far did Toshi drive along the third road?

Share

a) The first road is $2\frac{1}{4}$ km long and the second road is $1\frac{3}{8}$ km long.

Find $2\frac{1}{4} + 1\frac{3}{8}$.

I will add the wholes first and then add the parts.

Add the wholes first: $2 + 1 = 3$

Then add the parts: $\frac{1}{4} + \frac{3}{8}$

A common denominator is 8: $\frac{1}{4} = \frac{2}{8}$

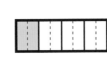

So $\frac{1}{4} + \frac{3}{8} = \frac{2}{8} + \frac{3}{8} = \frac{5}{8}$

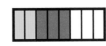

Add the wholes and the parts: $3 + \frac{5}{8} = 3\frac{5}{8}$

Toshi has driven $3\frac{5}{8}$ km in total along the two roads.

b) The total distance from work to home is $4\frac{1}{8}$ km. The first two roads added to $3\frac{5}{8}$ km.

Find the difference between $3\frac{5}{8}$ and $4\frac{1}{8}$.

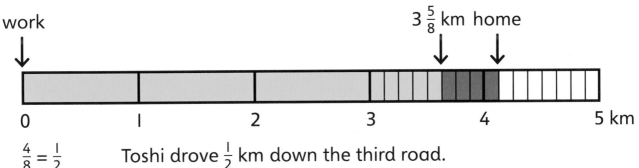

$\frac{4}{8} = \frac{1}{2}$ Toshi drove $\frac{1}{2}$ km down the third road.

109

Think together

1 Jen drives along two roads, as shown on the map.

What is the total distance she drives?

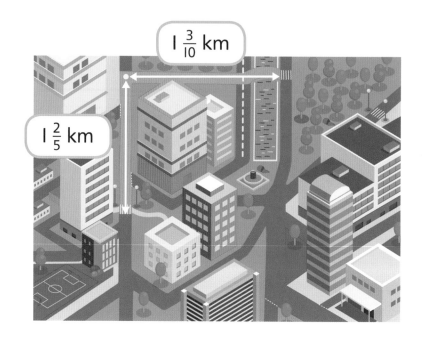

1 $\frac{3}{10}$ km

1 $\frac{2}{5}$ km

Add the wholes: 1 + 1 = ☐

Add the parts: $\frac{2}{5} + \frac{3}{10}$

$= \frac{\square}{10} + \frac{3}{10}$

$= \frac{\square}{10}$

Jen drives ☐ $\frac{\square}{\square}$ km in total.

1 $\frac{2}{5}$

1 $\frac{3}{10}$

2 Jen uses 2 $\frac{3}{4}$ litres of petrol to drive to work.

She uses $\frac{5}{12}$ of a litre of petrol to drive for lunch.

How many litres of petrol does she use in total?

Jen uses ☐ $\frac{\square}{\square}$ litres of petrol in total.

3 Luis was working on some fraction questions Mr Dean had set when the bell rang. Complete the missing steps.

a)

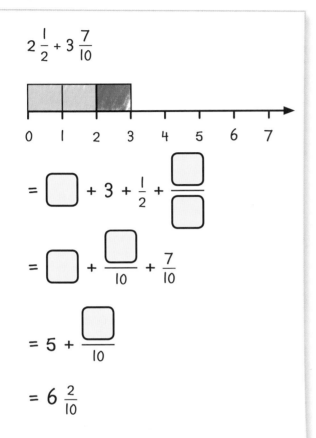

$2\frac{1}{2} + 3\frac{7}{10}$

$= \boxed{} + 3 + \frac{1}{2} + \frac{\boxed{}}{\boxed{}}$

$= \boxed{} + \frac{\boxed{}}{10} + \frac{7}{10}$

$= 5 + \frac{\boxed{}}{10}$

$= 6\frac{2}{10}$

b)

$\frac{7}{3} + \frac{5}{6}$

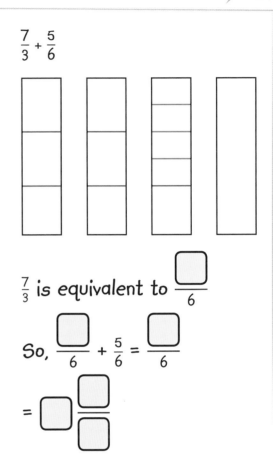

$\frac{7}{3}$ is equivalent to $\frac{\boxed{}}{6}$

So, $\frac{\boxed{}}{6} + \frac{5}{6} = \frac{\boxed{}}{6}$

$= \boxed{}\frac{\boxed{}}{\boxed{}}$

I will convert any improper fractions to mixed numbers.

I wonder if you have to do this for $\frac{7}{3} + \frac{5}{6}$.

c) Mr Dean has marked this question correct.

What fraction is covered by the eraser?

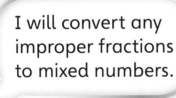

$1\frac{1}{8} + = 2\frac{11}{16}$

→ Practice book 5B p80

Adding fractions ③

Discover

1 **a)** Jamie pours her water into Andy's bucket.

Will the bucket overflow? Explain your answer.

b) How much water do they have altogether?

Share

a) Andy's bucket is $\frac{1}{3}$ full. Jamie's bucket is $\frac{4}{9}$ full. Work out $\frac{1}{3} + \frac{4}{9}$.

× 3

$$\frac{1}{3} = \frac{3}{9}$$

× 3

A common denominator of 3 and 9 is 9.

 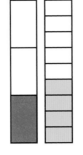 

So $\frac{1}{3} + \frac{4}{9} = \frac{3}{9} + \frac{4}{9} = \frac{7}{9}$

Because $\frac{7}{9} < 1$, Jamie's water will fit into Andy's bucket. The bucket will not overflow.

b) Altogether, they have $3\frac{1}{3} + 1\frac{4}{9}$ buckets of water.

$$3\frac{1}{3} = \frac{10}{3} \qquad\qquad 1\frac{4}{9} = \frac{13}{9}$$

> First I will convert each number to an improper fraction.

    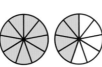

We now need to add $\frac{10}{3} + \frac{13}{9}$. First, find a common denominator.

× 3

$$\frac{10}{3} = \frac{30}{9}$$

× 3

So $3\frac{1}{3} + 1\frac{4}{9} = \frac{30}{9} + \frac{13}{9}$

$$= \frac{43}{9}$$

$$= 4\frac{7}{9}$$

> I know that $4 \times 9 = 36$, so 36 ninths make 4 wholes, with 7 ninths left over.

They have $4\frac{7}{9}$ buckets of water in total.

Think together

1 How much water do the children have in total?

This bucket is $\frac{3}{5}$ full.

Andy

This bucket is $\frac{3}{10}$ full.

Jamie

Convert each number to an improper fraction.

$2\frac{3}{5} = \dfrac{\boxed{}}{5}$

$4\frac{3}{10} = \dfrac{\boxed{}}{10}$

Find a common denominator:

$$\dfrac{\boxed{}}{5} = \dfrac{\boxed{}}{10}$$

So $2\frac{3}{5} + 4\frac{3}{10} = \dfrac{\boxed{}}{5} + \dfrac{\boxed{}}{10}$

$$= \dfrac{\boxed{}}{10} + \dfrac{\boxed{}}{10}$$

$$= \dfrac{\boxed{}}{10}$$

$$= \boxed{}\dfrac{\boxed{}}{10}$$

I wonder if I could use a different method to solve this.

2 Add together $2\frac{3}{4}$ and $\frac{5}{8}$.

$$2\frac{3}{4} + \frac{5}{8} = \boxed{}\,\frac{\boxed{}}{\boxed{}}$$

3 Andy and Jamie are solving some fraction addition problems.

CHALLENGE

I added the wholes and then added the parts.

Jamie

I converted each to an improper fraction first.

Andy

a) Use both methods to work out $2\frac{1}{4} + 1\frac{3}{20}$.

b) Use both methods to work out $1\frac{11}{15} + 2\frac{2}{3}$.

c) Which method did you prefer?

I think both methods are equally good.

I am not sure if I would use Andy's method to work out the second one.

115

→ Practice book 5B p83

Subtracting fractions ①

Discover

I have just $\frac{2}{5}$ of a litre of water left in my can.

There are $2\frac{9}{10}$ litres of water in mine.

Danny

Amelia

① a) Amelia waters some flowers.

   She uses $\frac{2}{10}$ of a litre of water from her watering can.

   How much water does she have left?

b) How much more water than Danny does Amelia have now?

Share

a) Amelia has $2\frac{9}{10}$ litres of water.

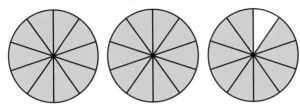

Amelia uses $\frac{2}{10}$ of a litre.

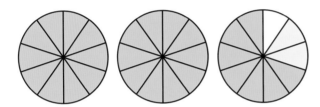

$2\frac{9}{10} - \frac{2}{10} = 2\frac{7}{10}$

Amelia has $2\frac{7}{10}$ litres of water left.

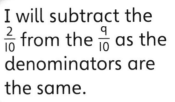

I will subtract the $\frac{2}{10}$ from the $\frac{9}{10}$ as the denominators are the same.

b) To work out the difference, subtract $\frac{2}{5}$ from $2\frac{7}{10}$.

I will convert $\frac{2}{5}$ to $\frac{4}{10}$ and then use a diagram to help me subtract this from $2\frac{7}{10}$.

Find a common denominator: $\frac{2}{5} = \frac{4}{10}$ ($\times 2$)

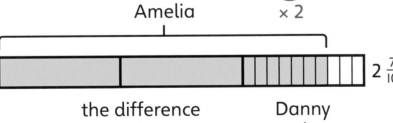

Amelia $\qquad 2\frac{7}{10}$

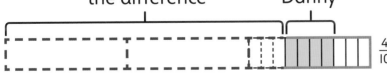

the difference $\qquad$ Danny $\qquad \frac{4}{10}$

$2\frac{7}{10} - \frac{4}{10} = 2\frac{3}{10}$

Amelia has $2\frac{3}{10}$ litres more water than Danny.

Think together

1 **a)** Use the diagram to help you work out $3\frac{7}{8} - \frac{2}{8}$.

$\dfrac{7}{8} - \dfrac{2}{8} = \dfrac{\boxed{}}{8}$

So, $3\dfrac{7}{8} - \dfrac{2}{8} = \boxed{}\dfrac{\boxed{}}{8}$

b) Use the diagram to help you work out $3\frac{7}{8} - \frac{3}{4}$.

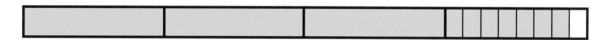

$3\dfrac{7}{8} - \dfrac{3}{4} = 3\dfrac{7}{8} - \dfrac{\boxed{}}{8}$

$= \boxed{}\dfrac{\boxed{}}{8}$

2 There are $4\frac{5}{6}$ pizzas.

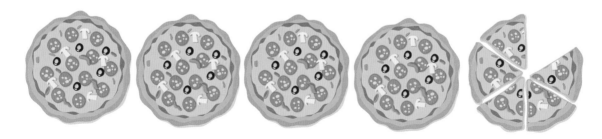

Max eats $\frac{1}{3}$ of a pizza. How much pizza is left?

There are $\boxed{}\dfrac{\boxed{}}{6}$ pizzas left.

3 **a)** Work out the answers to the following subtractions.

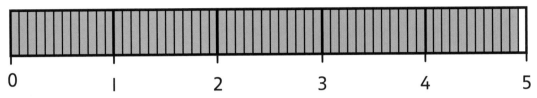

> I need to make sure that the denominators of the fractions are equal.

$4\frac{11}{12} - \frac{11}{12} = \boxed{}$

$4\frac{11}{12} - \frac{5}{6} = \boxed{}\frac{\boxed{}}{\boxed{}}$

$4\frac{11}{12} - \frac{3}{4} = \boxed{}\frac{\boxed{}}{\boxed{}}$

$4\frac{11}{12} - \frac{2}{3} = \boxed{}\frac{\boxed{}}{\boxed{}}$

$4\frac{11}{12} - \frac{1}{2} = \boxed{}\frac{\boxed{}}{\boxed{}}$

b) What patterns do you notice?

119

→ **Practice book 5B p86**

Subtracting fractions ❷

Discover

Start: $4\frac{1}{4}$ km Fun Run!

❶ **a)** Toshi has run $\frac{3}{4}$ km in the Fun Run.

How much further does he have to run to complete the Fun Run?

b) Toshi runs another $\frac{7}{8}$ km.

Now how much further does Toshi have to run to complete the Fun Run?

120

Share

a) The Fun Run is $4\frac{1}{4}$ km long. Toshi has run $\frac{3}{4}$ km, so find $4\frac{1}{4} - \frac{3}{4}$.

$4\frac{1}{4}$ is the equivalent to $3\frac{5}{4}$.

$3\frac{5}{4} - \frac{3}{4} = 3\frac{2}{4}$

$3\frac{2}{4} = 3\frac{1}{2}$

> I need to subtract $\frac{3}{4}$ from $4\frac{1}{4}$. I cannot subtract $\frac{3}{4}$ from $\frac{1}{4}$ without splitting one of the wholes.

> $3\frac{2}{4}$ can be simplified to $3\frac{1}{2}$.

Toshi has to run a further $3\frac{1}{2}$ km to complete the race.

b) Toshi runs another $\frac{7}{8}$ km.

$3\frac{1}{2} - \frac{7}{8}$

A common denominator is 8: $3\frac{1}{2} = 3\frac{4}{8}$

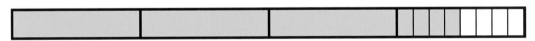

Split another whole into eighths: $3\frac{4}{8} = 2 + \frac{8}{8} + \frac{4}{8} = 2\frac{12}{8}$

$2\frac{12}{8} - \frac{7}{8} = 2\frac{5}{8}$

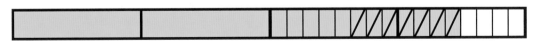

Toshi now has to run a further $2\frac{5}{8}$ km to complete the race.

Think together

1 The ribbon used to mark the finish line is $3\frac{1}{5}$ metres long.

$\frac{3}{5}$ metres of ribbon is cut off the end.

How long is the piece of ribbon now?

$3\frac{1}{5} - \frac{3}{5}$

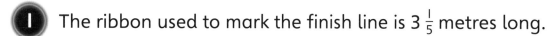

$3\frac{1}{5} = 2\frac{\Box}{5}$

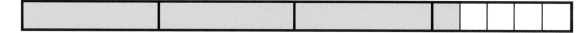

So $3\frac{1}{5} - \frac{3}{5} = 2\frac{\Box}{5} - \frac{3}{5}$

$= 2\frac{\Box}{5}$

2 Subtract $\frac{7}{10}$ from $3\frac{1}{2}$.

$\frac{1}{2} = \frac{\Box}{10}$ so $3\frac{1}{2} = 3\frac{\Box}{10} = 2\frac{\Box}{10}$

$3\frac{1}{2} - \frac{7}{10}$ is the same as $2\frac{\Box}{10} - \frac{7}{10} = \Box\frac{\Box}{10}$

$= \Box\frac{\Box}{5}$

3 Olivia is finding the answer to $2\frac{1}{4} - \frac{5}{8}$.

CHALLENGE

I subtracted $\frac{5}{8}$ from one of the wholes and got $\frac{3}{8}$.

I then added together $\frac{3}{8}$ and $\frac{1}{4}$ to get $\frac{5}{8}$.

I started with $2\frac{1}{4}$.

So the answer is $1\frac{5}{8}$ as there was a whole one left.

Does Olivia's method work?

Use a diagram to explain Olivia's method.

I will use a fraction strip to help me explain this method.

123

Subtracting fractions ❸

Discover

1 **a)** Is Kate's answer correct?

Explain Kate's method. Draw a diagram to explain.

b) Miss Hall now asks the children to work out $3\frac{1}{2} - 1\frac{3}{4}$.

Use a diagram to work out the answer.

Share

a) Kate starts with $3\frac{3}{4}$.

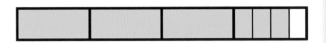

First Kate writes the fractions over the same denominator.

$1\frac{1}{2} = 1\frac{2}{4}$

Kate subtracts the wholes first.

$3 - 1 = 2$

wholes: $3 - 1 = 2$

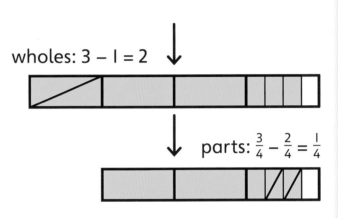

Kate then subtracts the parts.

$\frac{3}{4} - \frac{2}{4} = \frac{1}{4}$

parts: $\frac{3}{4} - \frac{2}{4} = \frac{1}{4}$

So, $3\frac{3}{4} - 1\frac{1}{2} = 3\frac{3}{4} - 1\frac{2}{4}$

$\qquad = 2\frac{1}{4}$

Kate's answer is correct.

b) Start with $3\frac{1}{2}$.

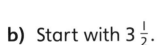

$3\frac{1}{2} - 1\frac{3}{4} = 3\frac{2}{4} - 1\frac{3}{4}$

$\qquad = 2\frac{6}{4} - 1\frac{3}{4}$

$\qquad = 1\frac{3}{4}$

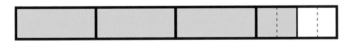

> I found a common denominator first. I needed to divide a whole into 4 quarters so I could do the subtraction.

Think together

1 Work out $3\frac{4}{5} - 1\frac{7}{10}$.

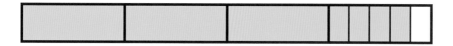

$3\frac{4}{5} = 3\frac{\boxed{}}{10}$

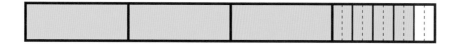

Subtract the wholes: $3 - 1 = \boxed{}$

Subtract the parts: $\dfrac{\boxed{}}{10} - \dfrac{7}{10} = \dfrac{\boxed{}}{10}$

$3\frac{4}{5} - 1\frac{7}{10} = \boxed{}\dfrac{\boxed{}}{10}$

2 Work out $4\frac{2}{9} - 2\frac{1}{3}$.

$2\frac{1}{3} = 2\frac{3}{9}$

$4\frac{2}{9} - 2\frac{3}{9} = 3\dfrac{\boxed{}}{9} - 2\frac{3}{9}$

$= \boxed{}\dfrac{\boxed{}}{9}$

3 Max is working out the answer to $4\frac{1}{2} - 1\frac{3}{4}$.

I subtract the 1 first.

$4\frac{1}{2} - 1 = 3\frac{1}{2}$

I now subtract the $\frac{3}{4}$.

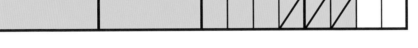

$3\frac{2}{4} - \frac{3}{4} = 2\frac{6}{4} - \frac{3}{4}$

$\qquad = 2\frac{3}{4}$

a) Use Max's method to work out $3\frac{7}{10} - 1\frac{1}{2}$.

b) Use Max's method to work out $10\frac{3}{8} - 4\frac{11}{16}$.

The last step of Max's method is similar to what we did in the last lesson when subtracting a proper fraction.

I wonder if Max's method always works.

→ **Practice book 5B p92**

Subtracting fractions ④

Discover

I have $4\frac{1}{2}$ packs of stickers.

Alex

My straw is $12\frac{3}{10}$ cm long.

Lexi

① a) Lexi uses $2\frac{1}{6}$ packs of stickers on her card.

How many packs of stickers does she have left?

b) Alex cuts off a piece of straw that is $2\frac{3}{5}$ cm long.

How long is the straw she has left?

Share

I will convert each number to an improper fraction and then subtract. I need to make sure the denominators are the same before I subtract.

a) Lexi started with $4\frac{1}{2}$ packs of stickers and used $2\frac{1}{6}$ packs, so find $4\frac{1}{2} - 2\frac{1}{6}$.

Convert mixed numbers to improper fractions:

$4\frac{1}{2} = \frac{9}{2}$

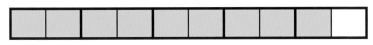

$2\frac{1}{6} = \frac{13}{6}$

$\times 3$

A common denominator is 6: $\quad \frac{9}{2} = \frac{27}{6}$

$\times 3$

$\frac{27}{6} - \frac{13}{6} = \frac{14}{6}$

Convert the answer back to a mixed number:

$\frac{14}{6} = 2\frac{2}{6} = 2\frac{1}{3}$

Lexi has $2\frac{1}{3}$ packs of stickers left.

b) $12\frac{3}{10} - 2\frac{3}{5}$

Change to improper fractions: $\qquad = \frac{123}{10} - \frac{13}{5}$

Make the denominators equal: $\qquad = \frac{123}{10} - \frac{26}{10}$

Subtract: $\qquad = \frac{97}{10}$

Convert back to a mixed number: $= 9\frac{7}{10}$ cm

The straw that Alex has left is $9\frac{7}{10}$ cm long.

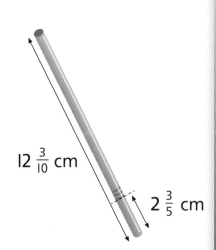

$12\frac{3}{10}$ cm

$2\frac{3}{5}$ cm

Think together

1 Lexi has some string which is $5\frac{1}{4}$ cm long. Lexi cuts off a piece that is $2\frac{7}{8}$ cm long.

How long is the string that is left?

$$5\frac{1}{4} - 2\frac{7}{8} = \frac{\boxed{}}{4} - \frac{\boxed{}}{8}$$

$$= \frac{\boxed{}}{8} - \frac{\boxed{}}{8}$$

$$= \frac{\boxed{}}{8}$$

$$= \boxed{}\frac{\boxed{}}{8}$$

2 **a)** Work out $2\frac{11}{12} - 2\frac{3}{4}$.

$$2\frac{11}{12} - 2\frac{3}{4} = \frac{\boxed{}}{\boxed{}} - \frac{\boxed{}}{\boxed{}} = \frac{\boxed{}}{\boxed{}}$$

How can you use your answer from part a) to work out these subtractions?

b) $3\frac{11}{12} - 2\frac{3}{4}$

c) $2\frac{11}{12} - 1\frac{3}{4}$

d) $12\frac{11}{12} - 2\frac{3}{4}$

e) $2\frac{10}{12} - 1$

3 Bella and Aki are working out this subtraction:

$96\frac{4}{9} - 85\frac{2}{3}$

I am going to convert each mixed number to an improper fraction.

I do not think this is the best method for these fractions.

Bella

Aki

a) Do you agree or disagree with Aki?

b) What is the answer to the question?

I am going to subtract the whole numbers first.

→ Practice book 5B p95

Problem solving – mixed word problems ❶

Discover

For these two dresses I used $1\frac{3}{5}$ metres of red ribbon and $2\frac{7}{10}$ metres of yellow ribbon.

Holly

❶ **a)** How much ribbon did Holly use in total to make the two dresses?

b) Holly used $4\frac{3}{4}$ metres of fabric for the dotty dress.

She used $2\frac{7}{20}$ metres of fabric for the stripy dress.

How much more dotty fabric did Holly use?

Share

a) Holly used $1\frac{3}{5}$ metres of red ribbon and $2\frac{7}{10}$ metres of yellow ribbon.

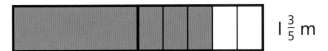 $1\frac{3}{5}$ m

 $2\frac{7}{10}$ m

Add the wholes: $1 + 2 = 3$

Add the parts: $\frac{3}{5} + \frac{7}{10}$

$\frac{3}{5} = \frac{6}{10}$

So, $\frac{3}{5} + \frac{7}{10} = \frac{6}{10} + \frac{7}{10}$

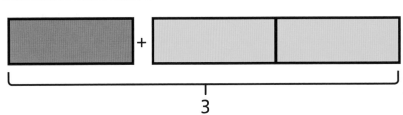

3

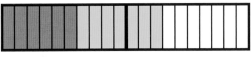

$\frac{6}{10}$ $+$ $\frac{7}{10}$ $=$ $\frac{13}{10} = 1\frac{3}{10}$

So $1\frac{3}{5} + 2\frac{7}{10} = 3 + 1\frac{3}{10} = 4\frac{3}{10}$

Holly used $4\frac{3}{10}$ metres of ribbon in total.

b) $4\frac{3}{4} - 2\frac{7}{20}$

$= 4\frac{15}{20} - 2\frac{7}{20}$

$= 2\frac{8}{20}$

$= 2\frac{2}{5}$

Holly used $2\frac{2}{5}$ metres more of the dotty fabric.

> To find the difference, I need to do a subtraction.

> First I write $4\frac{3}{4}$ as $4\frac{15}{20}$.
> Then I subtract the wholes and subtract the parts.

133

Think together

1 Holly makes a dressing gown and a pair of shorts.
She uses stripy fabric.

How much stripy fabric is needed in total
to make these two items?

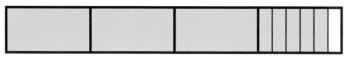 $3\frac{5}{6}$ m

 $\frac{1}{2}$ m

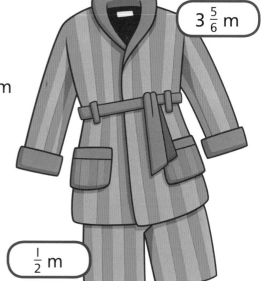

$3\frac{5}{6}$ m

$\frac{1}{2}$ m

Holly needs $\boxed{}\,\dfrac{\boxed{}}{\boxed{}}$ metres of stripy fabric.

2 Holly has $4\frac{11}{25}$ metres of ribbon.

She cuts the ribbon into two pieces. One piece is $2\frac{4}{5}$ m long.

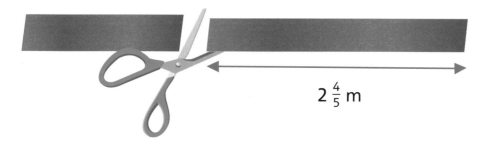

$2\frac{4}{5}$ m

How long is the other piece?

The other piece of ribbon is $\boxed{}\,\dfrac{\boxed{}}{\boxed{}}$ metres long.

3 The table shows the amount of dotty fabric Holly uses for four different items.

Item	Amount of fabric
	$3\frac{1}{2}$ metres
	$2\frac{9}{10}$ metres
	2 metres
	10 metres

How much fabric does Holly use in total?

I am not sure how to add these as some are just whole numbers.

I think you can add the dress and trousers together first and then add on the other whole metres.

135

Problem solving – mixed word problems ❷

Discover

Toshi

Jen

Milk

Milk

1 ½ litres

1 **a)** Jen pours 3 glasses of milk from the 1 $\frac{1}{2}$ litre carton.

   Each glass holds $\frac{1}{8}$ of a litre.

   How much milk is left in the carton?

b) The large carton holds 2 $\frac{3}{4}$ litres more than the small carton.

   How much milk do the two cartons hold in total?

Share

a) The carton holds $1\frac{1}{2}$ litres. Each glass holds $\frac{1}{8}$ litre.

Full carton

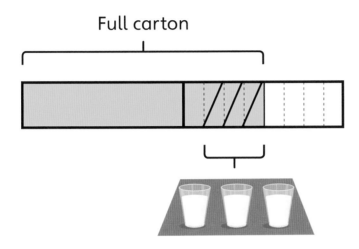

> I converted $1\frac{1}{2}$ to $1\frac{4}{8}$ to make it easier to subtract $\frac{3}{8}$.

$1\frac{4}{8} - \frac{3}{8} = 1\frac{1}{8}$. There is $1\frac{1}{8}$ litres of milk left in the carton.

b)

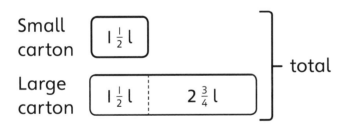

Small carton — $1\frac{1}{2}$ l

Large carton — $1\frac{1}{2}$ l : $2\frac{3}{4}$ l

total

> I worked out how much was in the large carton first and then added this on to the small carton.

Large carton

$1\frac{1}{2} + 2\frac{3}{4} = 1\frac{2}{4} + 2\frac{3}{4}$

Add the wholes: $1 + 2 = 3$

Add the parts: $\frac{2}{4} + \frac{3}{4} = \frac{5}{4} = 1\frac{1}{4}$

Add wholes and parts: $3 + 1\frac{1}{4} = 4\frac{1}{4}$

The large carton holds $4\frac{1}{4}$ litres.

Total

$1\frac{1}{2} + 4\frac{1}{4} = 1\frac{2}{4} + 4\frac{1}{4}$

$1 + 4 = 5$

$\frac{1}{2} + \frac{1}{4} = \frac{3}{4}$

$5 + \frac{3}{4} = 5\frac{3}{4}$

There are $5\frac{3}{4}$ litres of milk in total.

Think together

1 Kate has a bottle of apple juice.

The bottle holds $\frac{7}{10}$ of a litre.

Kate pours a glass of juice. The glass holds $\frac{1}{5}$ of a litre.

Kate pours $\frac{7}{20}$ of a litre into a jug.

How much apple juice is left in the bottle?

There are $\dfrac{\boxed{}}{\boxed{}}$ of a litre left in the bottle.

2 A, B and C are equally spaced. What number is the arrow at C pointing to?

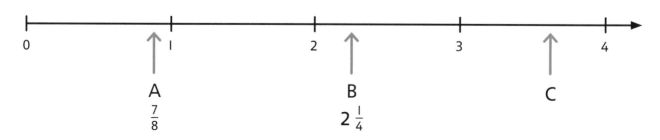

A
$\frac{7}{8}$

B
$2\frac{1}{4}$

C

The arrow at C is pointing to $\boxed{}\dfrac{\boxed{}}{\boxed{}}$.

CHALLENGE

3 **a)** What is the perimeter of this triangle?

$1\frac{1}{3}$ cm $2\frac{1}{6}$ cm

Not drawn to scale.

$3\frac{7}{12}$ cm

The perimeter of the triangle is ⬜ $\frac{⬜}{⬜}$ cm.

b) The perimeter of this triangle is 12 cm.

What is the missing length?

$5\frac{1}{2}$ cm

? cm

Not drawn to scale.

$5\frac{9}{20}$ cm

The missing length is ⬜ $\frac{⬜}{⬜}$ cm.

I wonder if I can add all three fractions together at once.

Remember, the perimeter of a shape is the distance all the way around.

139

End of unit check

1. What is $\frac{3}{5} + \frac{3}{5} + \frac{3}{5} + \frac{3}{5}$ equal to?

   A $\frac{12}{20}$ B $1\frac{2}{5}$ C $2\frac{2}{5}$ D $4\frac{3}{5}$

2. What is the missing number?

   $$\frac{2}{3} + \frac{\boxed{}}{18} = \frac{17}{18}$$

   A 5   B 6   C 15   D 17

3. Lee took part in a race. He ran for $\frac{3}{5}$ of the race, cycled for $\frac{3}{10}$ and swam for the rest. What fraction of the race did he swim for?

   A $\frac{6}{15}$ B $\frac{9}{10}$ C $\frac{1}{10}$ D $\frac{9}{15}$

4. What number is missing from the part-whole model?

   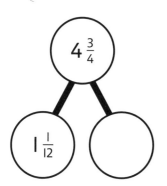

   A $3\frac{2}{3}$ B $3\frac{3}{4}$ C $5\frac{10}{11}$ D $3\frac{2}{8}$

5 What is $4\frac{1}{5} - \frac{7}{20}$?

A $4\frac{17}{20}$ **B** $3\frac{17}{20}$ **C** $4\frac{3}{20}$ **D** $3\frac{3}{20}$

6 The numbers on the cards increase by the same amount each time.

| | $3\frac{1}{8}$ | $4\frac{1}{2}$ | |

What numbers are on the two missing cards?

7 Three books are in a pile.

The first book has a thickness of $1\frac{1}{2}$ cm.

The second book has a thickness of $2\frac{1}{6}$ cm.

The total thickness of the books is 5 cm.

What is the thickness of the third book?

141

→ **Practice book 5B p104**

Unit 10
Fractions ③

In this unit we will …

- ⚡ Multiply proper fractions and mixed numbers by whole numbers
- ⚡ Find a fraction of an amount
- ⚡ Understand how fractions can be operators
- ⚡ Solve word problems involving fractions

How can you work out what each part is worth? How many yellow counters are there?

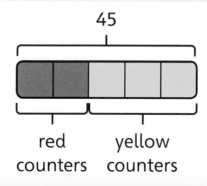

We will need some maths words. Do you know what all of these words mean?

multiply   proper fraction

improper fraction   mixed number

whole(s)   equal parts   divide

fraction of an amount   operator

numerator   denominator   convert

We will also need to represent fractions and mixed numbers using fraction strips. Use this model to work out $2\frac{1}{4} + 2\frac{2}{4}$.

Multiplying fractions ①

Discover

To make 1 milkshake:

$\frac{1}{5}$ of a jug of milk

10 strawberries

Blend together.

① **a)** What fraction of the jug of milk is needed for 3 milkshakes?

b) How many jugs of milk are needed to make 7 milkshakes?

Share

a) For 3 milkshakes, 3 lots of $\frac{1}{5}$ of a jug is needed.

I used addition. The denominators are the same, so I can just add the numerators.

$$\frac{1}{5} + \frac{1}{5} + \frac{1}{5} = \frac{3}{5}$$

Remember that $3 \times \frac{1}{5}$ is the same as $\frac{1}{5} \times 3$.

I used multiplication.

$$3 \times \frac{1}{5} = \frac{3}{5}$$

$\frac{3}{5}$ of the jug of milk is needed to make 3 milkshakes.

b)

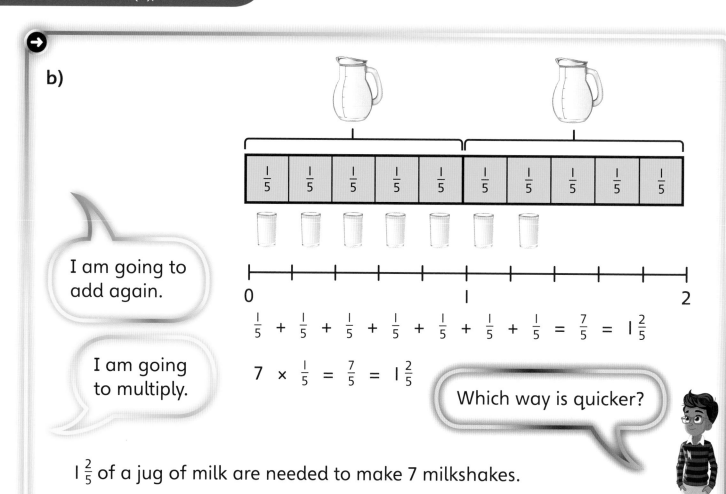

I am going to add again.

I am going to multiply.

Which way is quicker?

$$\frac{1}{5} + \frac{1}{5} + \frac{1}{5} + \frac{1}{5} + \frac{1}{5} + \frac{1}{5} + \frac{1}{5} = \frac{7}{5} = 1\frac{2}{5}$$

$$7 \times \frac{1}{5} = \frac{7}{5} = 1\frac{2}{5}$$

$1\frac{2}{5}$ of a jug of milk are needed to make 7 milkshakes.

Think together

1 A cat eats $\frac{1}{7}$ of a bag of cat food each day.

What fraction of the bag does the cat need for 4 days?

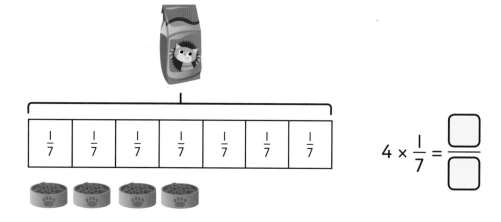

$$4 \times \frac{1}{7} = \frac{\boxed{}}{\boxed{}}$$

2 One glass holds $\frac{1}{8}$ of a bottle of orange juice.

How many bottles do you need for 11 glasses?

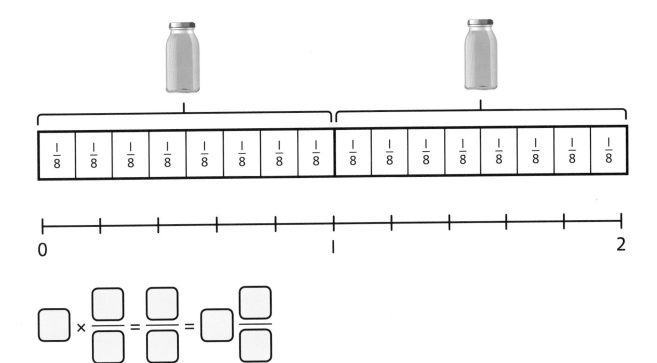

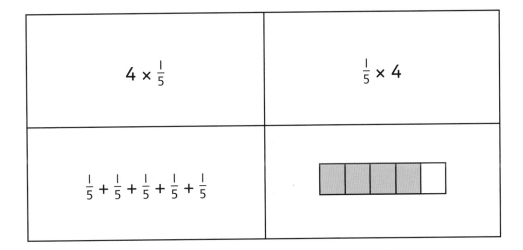

3 **a)** Do all of the following show $\frac{4}{5}$?

$4 \times \frac{1}{5}$	$\frac{1}{5} \times 4$
$\frac{1}{5} + \frac{1}{5} + \frac{1}{5} + \frac{1}{5} + \frac{1}{5}$	

b) Find 4 ways of showing $\frac{5}{8}$.

→ **Practice book 5B p107**

Multiplying fractions ②

Discover

1 **a)** What fraction of the box is needed each day for the 3 dogs?

b) How many boxes of dog food will Lexi and her mum need to buy to feed the dogs for 5 days?

Share

a) Each dog needs $\frac{2}{9}$ of the box. There are 3 dogs.

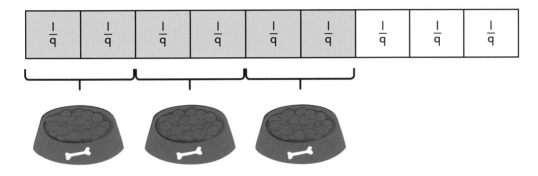

Using addition: $\quad \frac{2}{9} + \frac{2}{9} + \frac{2}{9} = \frac{6}{9} = \frac{2}{3}$

Using multiplication: $\quad \frac{2}{9} \times 3 = \frac{6}{9} = \frac{2}{3}$

$\frac{2}{3}$ of the box is needed each day for the 3 dogs.

b) Each day the dogs need $\frac{2}{3}$ of a box.

There are 5 days.

$\frac{2}{3} \times 5 = \frac{10}{3} = 3\frac{1}{3}$

> I think it is simpler to multiply. To work out how many $\frac{1}{3}$s, I work out $2 \times 5 = 10$.

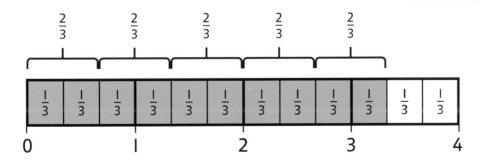

The dogs need $3\frac{1}{3}$ boxes for 5 days. Lexi and her mum will need to buy 4 boxes to feed the dogs for 5 days.

Think together

1 **a)** Lexi and her mum each eat $\frac{3}{7}$ of a bar of chocolate.

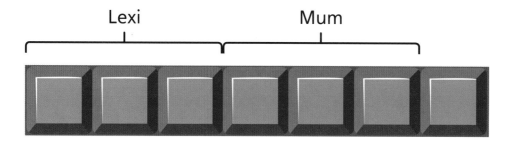

Lexi   Mum

What fraction of the chocolate bar do they eat in total?

$$\frac{3}{7} \times 2 = \frac{\boxed{}}{7}$$

In total, they eat $\frac{\boxed{}}{7}$ of the chocolate bar.

b) A bowl contains $\frac{2}{5}$ l of water.

How much water is there in 3 bowls?

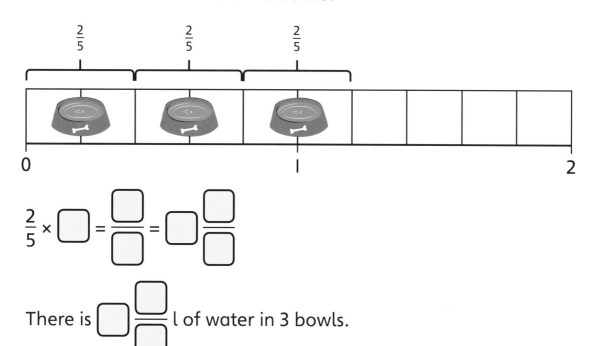

$$\frac{2}{5} \times \boxed{} = \frac{\boxed{}}{\boxed{}} = \boxed{} \frac{\boxed{}}{\boxed{}}$$

There is $\boxed{} \frac{\boxed{}}{\boxed{}}$ l of water in 3 bowls.

2 Kate runs around a circular track.

One lap is $\frac{3}{10}$ of a kilometre.

Kate runs 5 laps. How far does Kate run?

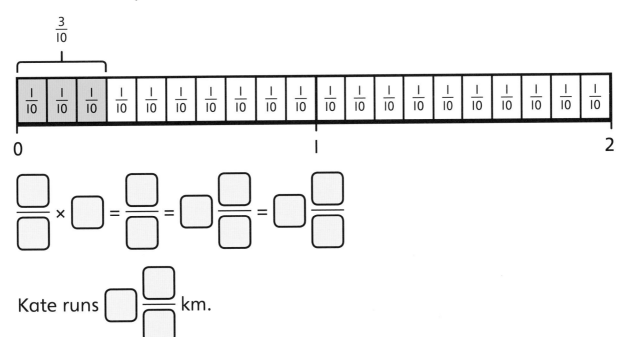

$$\frac{\square}{\square} \times \square = \frac{\square}{\square} = \square\frac{\square}{\square} = \square\frac{\square}{\square}$$

Kate runs $\square\frac{\square}{\square}$ km.

3 Work out the answers to each of the following questions.

Set A	Set B	Set C
$\frac{1}{5} \times 2$	$1 \times \frac{3}{8}$	$\frac{3}{4} \times 4$
$\frac{2}{5} \times 2$	$2 \times \frac{3}{8}$	$\frac{2}{5} \times 5$
$\frac{3}{5} \times 2$	$3 \times \frac{3}{8}$	$\frac{5}{6} \times 6$
$\frac{4}{5} \times 2$	$5 \times \frac{3}{8}$	$7 \times \frac{3}{7}$

> I have found a way to answer these questions without drawing a diagram each time.

Explain your method to a friend.

What do you notice about the answers to Set C?

151

→ Practice book 5B p110

Multiplying fractions ❸

Discover

Soup Challenge

For one pot of soup:

$1\frac{1}{6}$ jugs of stock

$1\frac{1}{2}$ onions

$3\frac{1}{4}$ potatoes

❶ a) 5 children take part in the Soup Challenge.

How many jugs of stock do the children use in total?

b) How many onions do the children use in total?

Share

a) 5 children use $1\frac{1}{6}$ jugs of stock each.

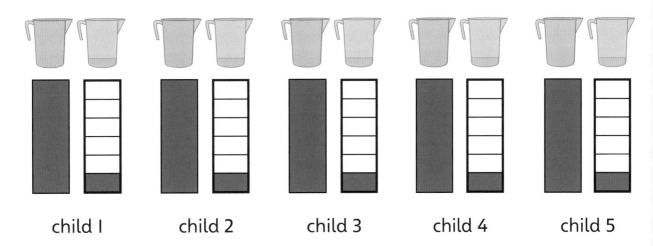

child 1   child 2   child 3   child 4   child 5

I will multiply the wholes first, then the fractions. Then I can add the answers together to find the total!

Multiply the wholes:

$1 × 5 = 5$

Multiply the parts:

$\frac{1}{6} × 5 = \frac{5}{6}$

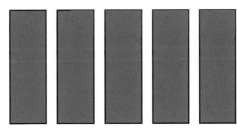

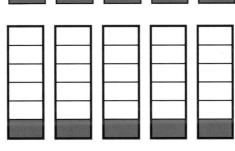

Add to find the total: $5 + \frac{5}{6} = 5\frac{5}{6}$

The children use $5\frac{5}{6}$ jugs of stock in total.

b) Each child needs $1\frac{1}{2}$ onions.

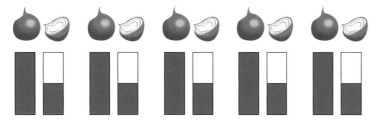

Multiply the wholes: $1 \times 5 = 5$

Multiply the parts: $\frac{1}{2} \times 5 = \frac{5}{2} = 2\frac{1}{2}$

Add together: $5 + 2\frac{1}{2} = 7\frac{1}{2}$

The children use $7\frac{1}{2}$ onions in total.

I will convert the improper fraction into a mixed number to make it easier to add.

Think together

1 Each child also needs $3\frac{1}{4}$ potatoes. How many potatoes are needed in total?

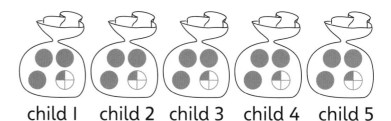

child 1   child 2   child 3   child 4   child 5

Multiply the wholes: $\boxed{} \times 5 = \boxed{}$

Multiply the parts: $\dfrac{\boxed{}}{\boxed{}} \times 5 = \dfrac{\boxed{}}{\boxed{}} = \boxed{}\dfrac{\boxed{}}{\boxed{}}$

Add together: $\boxed{} + \boxed{}\dfrac{\boxed{}}{\boxed{}} = \boxed{}\dfrac{\boxed{}}{\boxed{}}$

The children need $\boxed{}\dfrac{\boxed{}}{\boxed{}}$ potatoes in total.

2 **a)** Work out $1\frac{2}{5} \times 4$.

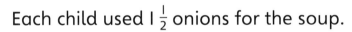

b) Explain how you can use your answer to work out these multiplications.

$2\frac{2}{5} \times 4$ $\qquad\qquad\qquad$ $1\frac{2}{5} \times 5$

3 Mrs Dean gave 4 onions to each of the 5 children.

Each child used $1\frac{1}{2}$ onions for the soup.

How many onions are left over in total?

I will use my answer from earlier and subtract.

I will work out how many each child has left over and then multiply by 5.

155

Multiplying fractions ④

Discover

Glacier

The glacier moves $1\frac{3}{4}$ yards each day

Yards are a unit of measure. We do not use these as much now.

1 a) How far does the glacier travel in 3 days?

b) How many days will it take the glacier to travel more than 15 yards?

Share

a) The glacier moves $1\frac{3}{4}$ yards each day.

Multiply $1\frac{3}{4}$ by 3 to work out how far it moves in 3 days.

day 1

day 2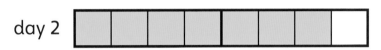

day 3

> I converted $1\frac{3}{4}$ to an improper fraction. I then multiplied by 3.

$1\frac{3}{4} = \frac{7}{4}$

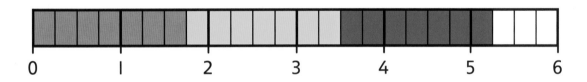

$$\frac{7}{4} \times 3 = \frac{21}{4} = 5\frac{1}{4}$$

The glacier travels $5\frac{1}{4}$ yards in 3 days.

b) Multiply $\frac{7}{4}$ by different numbers until the answer is greater than 15.

$$\frac{7}{4} \times 6 = \frac{42}{4} = 10\frac{2}{4}$$

$$\frac{7}{4} \times 7 = \frac{49}{4} = 12\frac{1}{4}$$

$$\frac{7}{4} \times 8 = \frac{56}{4} = 14$$

$$\frac{7}{4} \times 9 = \frac{63}{4} = 15\frac{3}{4}$$

> I used trial and error to find the correct answer.

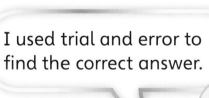

After 9 days, the glacier has moved more than 15 yards.

A different method:

How many $\frac{1}{4}$ in 15 yards? $15 \times 4 = 60$.

So, 15 yards is the same as 60 quarters or $\frac{60}{4}$ yards.

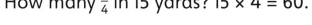

Every day, the glacier travels $\frac{7}{4}$ yards.

$$\frac{7}{4} \times ? > 15 \quad = \quad \frac{7}{4} \times ? > \frac{60}{4}$$

The missing number must be 9, because 7×9 is 63 and this is the first number in the 7 times-table that is greater than 60.

After 9 days, the glacier has moved more than 15 yards.

> I compared fractions to work out what I need to multiply by.

Think together

1 Olivia runs $2\frac{1}{3}$ km every hour. How far does she run in 4 hours?

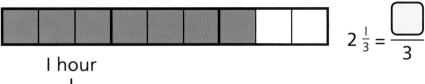

I hour

$2\frac{1}{3} = \dfrac{\boxed{}}{3}$

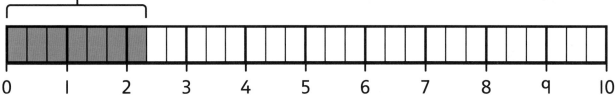

$$\frac{\boxed{}}{3} \times 4 = \frac{\boxed{}}{3} = \boxed{}\,\frac{\boxed{}}{3}$$

Olivia runs $\boxed{}\dfrac{\boxed{}}{\boxed{}}$ km.

2 **a)** Kate has worked out $1\frac{3}{5} \times 4$.

Explain Kate's method to a friend. You can use diagrams to help you explain, if necessary.

$$1\frac{3}{5} \times 4$$

$$1\frac{3}{5} = \frac{8}{5}$$

$$\frac{8}{5} \times 4 = \frac{32}{5}$$

$$\frac{32}{5} = 6\frac{2}{5}$$

b) Use Kate's method to work out $3\frac{1}{2} \times 5$ and $9 \times 1\frac{1}{10}$.

3 Here are some fractions and whole numbers.

CHALLENGE

$$1\frac{1}{3} \qquad 2\frac{1}{3} \qquad 3\frac{2}{3} \qquad 3\frac{1}{4}$$

$$3 \qquad\quad 6 \qquad\quad 9 \qquad\quad 12$$

Multiply each of the fractions in the top row by each number in the bottom row. Do you notice any patterns?

You can use the method from this lesson or the last lesson to help you.

159

Calculating fractions of amounts

Discover

1 **a)** There are 320 people in the theme park.

$\frac{2}{5}$ of the people are adults.

How many children are in the theme park?

b) A child ticket is $\frac{3}{8}$ of the cost of an adult ticket.

How much does an adult ticket cost?

Share

I drew a bar model to help me represent the situation. 2 parts represent the adults and 3 parts represent the children.

a) There are 320 people in the theme park.

$\frac{2}{5}$ of the people are adults.

This means $\frac{3}{5}$ of the people are children.

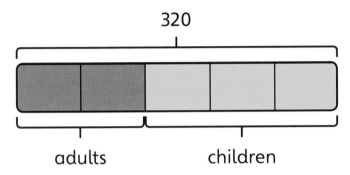

320

adults   children

Work out the value of $\frac{1}{5}$ by dividing 320 by 5.

$$5 \overline{\smash{\big)}\, 3\ ^32\ ^20} \quad \begin{array}{cc} 6 & 4 \end{array} \longrightarrow 320 \div 5 = 64$$

To work out the number of children multiply by 3.

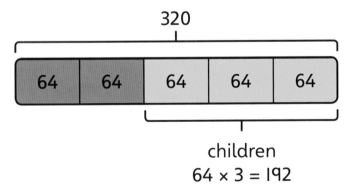

320

| 64 | 64 | 64 | 64 | 64 |

children

$64 \times 3 = 192$

There are 192 children in the theme park.

$\frac{3}{5}$ of the people are children, so I multiplied by 3 to work out $\frac{3}{5}$.

I worked out the number of adults and subtracted it from 320. You did it using a more efficient method.

b) A child ticket costs $\frac{3}{8}$ of an adult ticket.

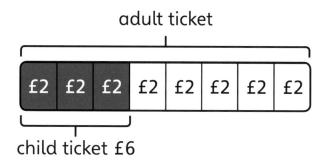

adult ticket

child ticket £6

Find out the value of $\frac{1}{8}$ by dividing the child cost by 3:   £6 ÷ 3 = £2

To find the cost of an adult ticket, multiply by 8:   £2 × 8 = £16

An adult ticket costs £16.

Think together

1 There are 78 people on the roller coaster.

$\frac{1}{6}$ of the people are under 16 years old.

How many people are 16 years or over?

78

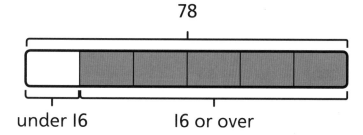

under 16   16 or over

$\boxed{} \div 6 = \boxed{}$

$\boxed{} \times \boxed{} = \boxed{}$

There are $\boxed{}$ people 16 years or over.

2 Max spends $\frac{7}{10}$ of his time at the theme park in queues.

Max spends 210 minutes queueing.

How long does he spend at the park altogether?

Max spends ☐ minutes at the theme park.

CHALLENGE

3 The pictogram shows the ratings for the theme park on the internet.

5 stars	😀 😀 😀
4 stars	😀 😀 😀 😀 😀 😀 😀 😀
3 stars	😀 😀 😀 😀 😀
2 stars	😀 😀 😀
1 star	😀

1,680 people have given the theme park 4 stars.

How many people gave the theme park 2 stars or less?

I worked out what one symbol represents by dividing, and then I multiplied.

I noticed something about the number of people who gave 4 stars and those that gave 2 stars or less.

163

→ Practice book 5B p119

Using fractions as operators

Discover

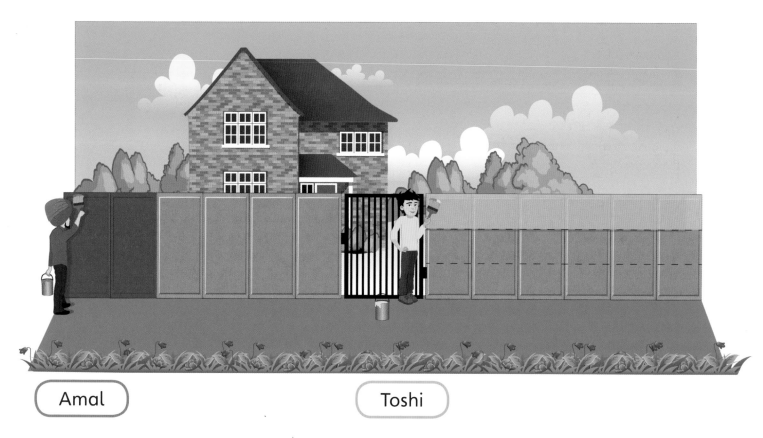

Amal

Toshi

I **a)** Who has painted $\frac{1}{3}$ of 6?

Who has painted $\frac{1}{3} \times 6$?

b) Who has painted the greatest amount of the fence?

What is the same and what is different about these calculations?

Share

a) Amal has painted 2 out of 6 panels.

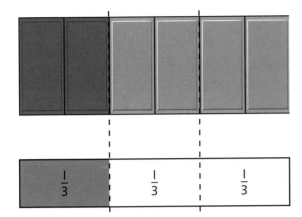

$\frac{2}{6} = \frac{1}{3}$

Amal has painted $\frac{1}{3}$ of 6.

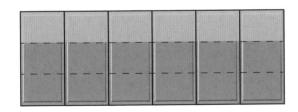

Toshi has painted $\frac{1}{3}$ of each of the 6 panels.

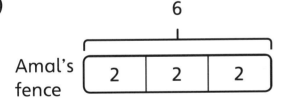

Toshi has painted $\frac{1}{3} \times 6$.

b)

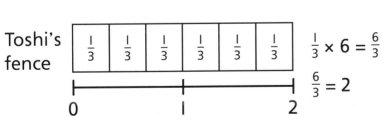

$6 \div 3 = 2$

So $\frac{1}{3}$ of $6 = 2$

$\frac{1}{3} \times 6 = \frac{6}{3}$

$\frac{6}{3} = 2$

The answers are the same, so $\frac{1}{3}$ of 6 is the same as saying $\frac{1}{3} \times 6$.

They have both painted the same amount of the fence.

One calculation involves dividing 6 into 3, the other involves multiplying $\frac{1}{3}$ by 6.

Think together

1 **a)** Amal is painting another fence. He needs to paint $\frac{2}{5}$ of these panels.

How many panels does he need to paint in total?

15

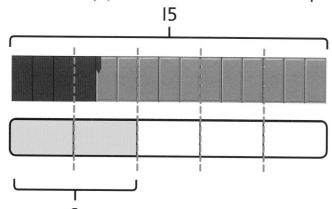

?

$15 \div 5 = \boxed{}$

$\boxed{} \times 2 = \boxed{}$

So $\frac{1}{5}$ of 15 = $\boxed{}$

So $\frac{2}{5}$ of 15 = $\boxed{}$

Amal needs to paint $\boxed{}$ panels in total.

b) Toshi paints $\frac{2}{5}$ of each panel. How many panels has he painted in total?

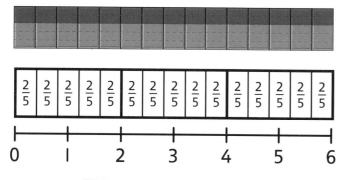

| $\frac{2}{5}$ | $\frac{2}{5}$ | $\frac{2}{5}$ | $\frac{2}{5}$ | $\frac{2}{5}$ | $\frac{2}{5}$ | $\frac{2}{5}$ | $\frac{2}{5}$ | $\frac{2}{5}$ | $\frac{2}{5}$ | $\frac{2}{5}$ | $\frac{2}{5}$ | $\frac{2}{5}$ | $\frac{2}{5}$ | $\frac{2}{5}$ |

0   1   2   3   4   5   6

$\frac{2}{5} \times 15 = \dfrac{\boxed{}}{15} = \boxed{}$

Toshi has painted $\boxed{}$ panels in total.

2 Which calculations will give the same answer?

$\frac{1}{10} \times 120$ $\frac{3}{4}$ of 24

$\frac{3}{4} \times 24$ $\frac{2}{3}$ of 84

$84 \times \frac{2}{3}$ $\frac{1}{10}$ of 120

---

3 Olivia and Mo are working out some calculations.

CHALLENGE

a) Olivia is working out $\frac{3}{4} \times 24$.

Olivia

I can think of this as being the same as $\frac{3}{4}$ of 24.

Use Olivia's method to work out $\frac{3}{4} \times 24$.

b) Mo is working out $\frac{1}{3}$ of 7.

Mo

I can think of this as being the same as $\frac{1}{3} \times 7$.

Use Mo's method to work out $\frac{1}{3} \times 7$.

I wonder why Olivia and Mo have chosen these methods.

I think they have chosen the most efficient way of working out their calculation.

→ **Practice book 5B p122**

Problem solving – mixed word problems

Discover

I have $\frac{7}{10}$ of the coins from the bag.

Mrs Dean

I have the rest of the coins.

Roman History Day

Roman coins

Max

Reena

1 **a)** Reena gives Max 18 coins. They now have the same number of coins. How many coins were in the bag?

b) How many coins did Reena have at the start?

Share

a) Reena has $\frac{7}{10}$ of the coins.

Max has the rest of the coins, so Max has $\frac{3}{10}$ of the coins.

I am going to draw a bar model to represent how many coins they each have.

Reena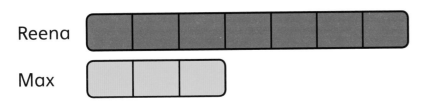

Max

Reena gives Max some coins, so they now have the same amount.

Reena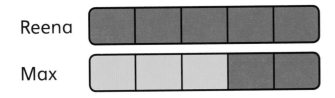

Max

I moved 2 of the parts to Max from Reena, so that they now have the same amount.

Reena gives Max 18 coins, so these 2 parts are equal to 18.

Reena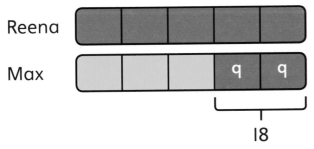

Max

18

I divided by 2 to work out 1 part and multiplied by 10 to find the total number of coins.

$18 \div 2 = 9$

So each part is worth 9 coins.

There are 10 parts in total.

$9 \times 10 = 90$

There were 90 coins in the bag.

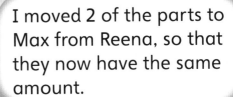

b) Each part is equal to 9.

Reena had 7 parts at the start.

$7 \times 9 = 63$

Reena had 63 coins at the start.

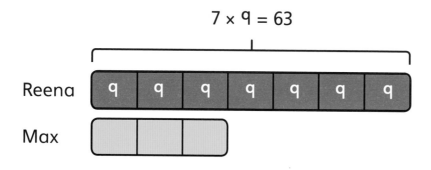

$7 \times 9 = 63$

Reena

Max

Think together

1 The class is split into 2 teams.

- $\frac{3}{5}$ of the class are in Team A.

- The rest of the class are in Team B.

- There are 6 more children in Team A.

How many children are there in the class?

Draw your own bar model. Now look at the information you know and write it on to help you work out what calculation you need to do.

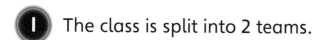

Team A

Team B

There are ☐ children in the class.

2 Mrs Dean has a bag of paper shapes.

She gives Max 120 shapes.

She has $\frac{2}{7}$ of the bag of shapes left.

How many paper shapes are there in total?

There are ☐ paper shapes in total.

3 Olivia has $\frac{1}{2}$ as many stickers as Zac.

Zac has $\frac{1}{3}$ as many stickers as Lexi.

There are 72 stickers in total.

How many stickers does Lexi have?

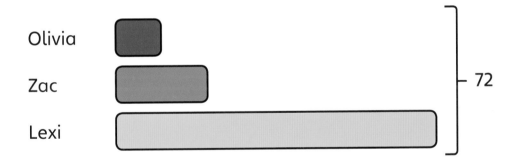

Lexi has ☐ stickers.

I used a bar model to help me. I need to split the bars into equal parts.

→ **Practice book 5B p125**

End of unit check

1 What is $\frac{1}{8} \times 3$?

A $\frac{3}{8}$ **B** $\frac{1}{24}$ **C** 24 **D** $\frac{3}{24}$

2 What is the missing number?

$\frac{2}{9} \times 5 = \frac{1}{9} \times \boxed{}$

A $\frac{10}{9}$ **B** $\frac{5}{9}$ **C** 10 **D** 5

3 A bag contains $1\frac{1}{4}$ kg of potatoes.

What is the total weight of 5 bags of potatoes?

A $\frac{5}{4}$ **B** $5\frac{1}{4}$ **C** 6 **D** $6\frac{1}{4}$

4 A box contains red and yellow counters.

There are 72 counters in the box.

$\frac{3}{8}$ of the counters are red.

How many yellow counters are in the box?

A $\frac{5}{8}$ **B** 27   **C** 45   **D** 72

5 Complete the statement.

$\frac{1}{3} \times 5 = \frac{1}{3}$ of $\boxed{}$

A $\frac{5}{3}$ **B** $1\frac{2}{3}$ **C** 5   **D** $\frac{5}{9}$

6 In the morning Lee eats $\frac{5}{6}$ of a packet of nuts.

In the afternoon he eats $\frac{1}{2}$ of what is left.

The bag contained 144 nuts.

How many nuts does he have left?

7 $\frac{2}{3}$ of a number is 18.

What is $\frac{5}{9}$ of the number?

→ **Practice book 5B p128**

Unit 11
Decimals and percentages

In this unit we will …

⚡ Read and write decimals up to three decimal places, including numbers greater than 1

⚡ Round decimals to nearest whole number and to one decimal place

⚡ Order and compare decimal numbers up to three decimal places

⚡ Write percentages as fractions and as decimals.

Do you remember what this is called? We use it to understand the place value of digits in a number.

How would you place 0·034 into the grid?

O	•	Tth	Hth	Thths
	•			

We will need some maths words.
Do you know what they all mean?

decimal   decimal place   tenths

hundredths   thousandths   decimal point

place value   digits   fractions

per cent (%)   percentages

We need to use the number line too.
Use it to help you show equivalent
fractions, decimals and percentages.

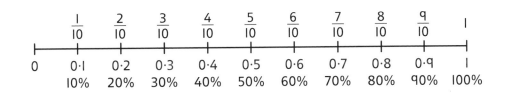

Writing decimals ❶

Discover

❶ a) Decide which one is the 'Odd one out'. Which number is different? Explain why.

b) Explain how to change the odd one out so it matches the other number representations.

Share

a) This number line counts up in tenths. The arrow points to 0·3.

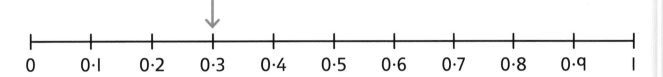

Each of these representations shows 3 tenths and 5 hundredths.

O	•	Tth	Hth
0	•	3	5

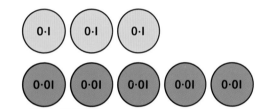

These both show 'Zero point thirty-five'.

We do not say 'Zero point thirty-five'. We say each number after the decimal point separately. So we say 'Zero point three five'.

0·3 is different from the other numbers, which show 0·35.

b) To show 0·35 on the number line, move the arrow half-way between 0·3 and 0·4.

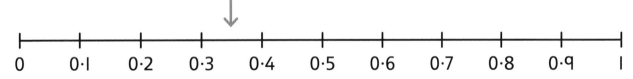

You can represent this on a different number line like this:

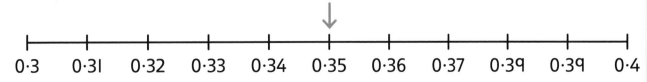

Think together

1 What numbers are shown on these number lines?

a)

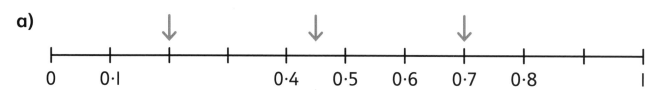

0   0·1   0·4   0·5   0·6   0·7   0·8   1

b)

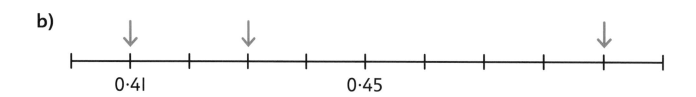

0·41   0·45

2 Show these numbers on a number line.

a)

two-tenths

c)

O	•	Tth	Hth
0	•	2	5

b)

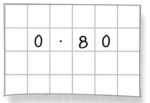
0 · 8 0

d)

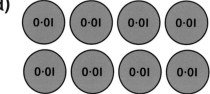
0·01 0·01 0·01 0·01
0·01 0·01 0·01 0·01

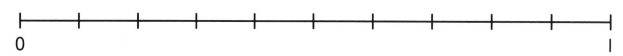

0   1

I wonder if 0·80 is the same as 0·8 or 0·08.

3 Molly thinks she has represented 0·6 using cubes on a place value grid.

a) Explain her mistake.

b) Find all the decimal numbers between 0 and 1 you can make using 6 cubes on a place value grid.

O	•	Tth	Hth
0	•		

Show each number on a number line. For example here is 0·42:

I will show them all on the same number line. I will have to approximate carefully.

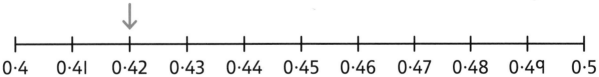

I will show them all on separate number lines so I can be exact.

179

→ **Practice book 5B p130**

Writing decimals ②

Discover

Isla

Bella

1 **a)** What is Isla's score?

b) Bella scores 1·45.

Represent this number in different ways.

Share

a) Isla's score is between 1 and 2.

I will count each interval on the number line.

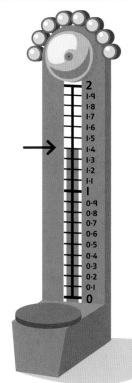

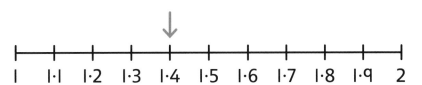

The scale is divided into tenths. Isla's score is 1·4.

b) Bella's score is 1·45. This is half-way between 1·4 and 1·5.

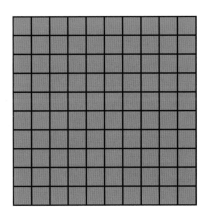

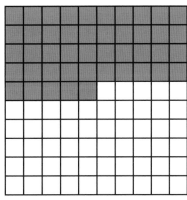

I can represent 1·45 in different ways.

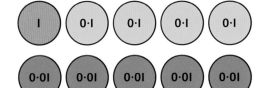

1·45

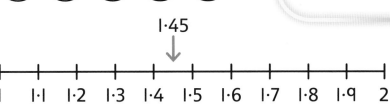

Think together

1 Who has a score of 2·05?

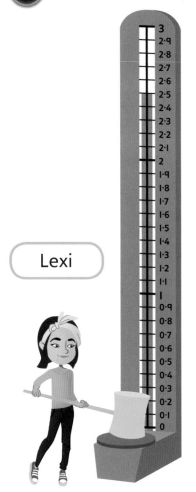

Lexi

Andy

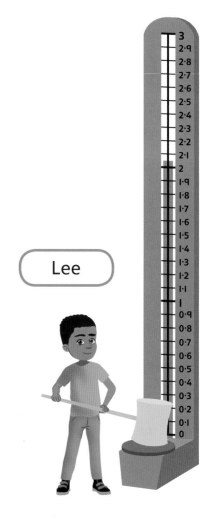

Lee

2 Show each of these numbers on a number line.

a)

O	•	Tth	Hth
① ①	•		0·01 0·01 0·01

b)

| 1 | 0·1 | 0·1 | 0·1 | 0·01 | 0·01 | 0·01 |

c)

O	•	Tth	Hth
2	•	3	0

CHALLENGE

3 Ebo and Kate are counting in tenths. Explain and correct their mistakes.

a)

1·6, 1·7, 1·8, 1·9, 1·10, 1·11

Ebo

b)

2·3, 2·2, 2·1, 2·09, 2·08, 2·07

Kate

I can show the mistakes using place value counters and exchange.

I will show the mistakes by writing the numbers in a place value grid.

183

Decimals as fractions ❶

Discover

Sofia

❶ **a)** Where is Sofia on the route planner? Find the location on the route planner, and describe it as a fraction of a kilometre.

b) After 15 minutes Sofia has run 1·5 km. Locate her position on the route planner, and describe it as a fraction.

Share

a) 0·5 is equivalent to one half.

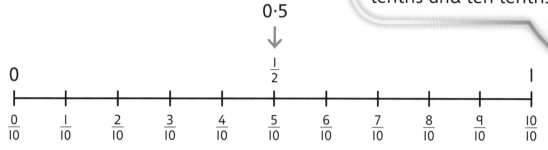

0·5 is equivalent to a half, because five tenths is half-way between zero tenths and ten tenths.

I think you could also write her distance as $\frac{5}{10}$ km, because $\frac{5}{10}$ is equivalent to $\frac{1}{2}$.

O	•	Tth
0	•	5

Sofia has run 0·5 km, which can also be written as $\frac{1}{2}$ km.

b)

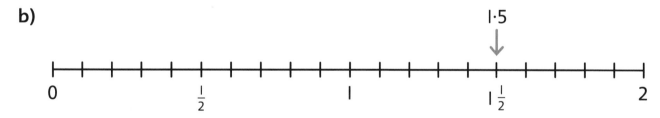

1·5 is equivalent to $1\frac{1}{2}$ and $1\frac{5}{10}$.

Think together

1 Jamie ran 0·7 km. Write this as a fraction.

O	•	Tth
	•	

I will use counters on a place value grid to help me.

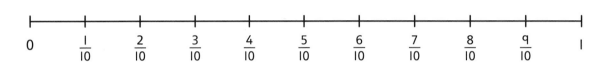

0    $\frac{1}{10}$ $\frac{2}{10}$ $\frac{3}{10}$ $\frac{4}{10}$ $\frac{5}{10}$ $\frac{6}{10}$ $\frac{7}{10}$ $\frac{8}{10}$ $\frac{9}{10}$ 1

I will use a number line to work it out.

0·7 km as a fraction is $\dfrac{\square}{\square}$ km.

2 These are the results for some other runners. Complete the table.

Runner	Distance as a decimal	Distance as a fraction
Aki	0·6 km	$\square$ km
Richard	$\square$ km	$\frac{3}{10}$ km
Jamilla	$\square$ km	$2\frac{3}{10}$ km
Kate	$\square$ km	$3\frac{1}{2}$ km

3 **a)** Write the distances shown on the route planner as decimals.

b) How far has the jogger run between B and C and C and D?

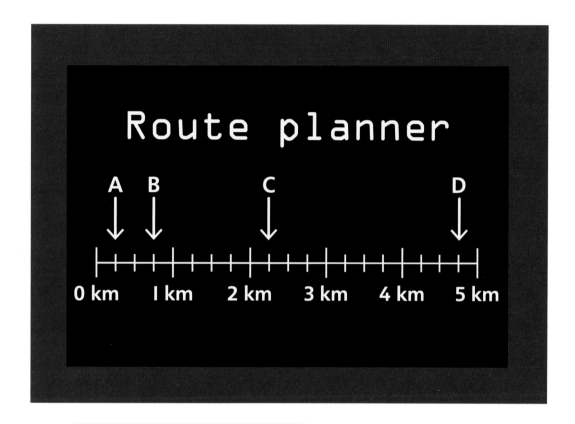

I think these are at $\frac{1}{4}$ and $\frac{3}{4}$ marks. I think these are written 1·4 and $\frac{3}{4}$. Am I right?

I think it helps to draw number lines marked in tenths.

$\frac{1}{4}$ is between 0·2 and 0·3.

→ **Practice book 5B p136**

Decimals as fractions ❷

Discover

1 a) Write the memory required for the games app as a fraction.

b) Write the memory required for the music app as a fraction in two different ways. Explain your answer.

Share

a) The games app requires 0·08 GB.

I can show this on a place value grid and a hundredths grid.

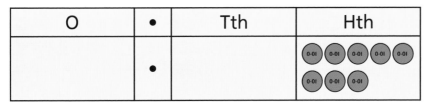

0·08 is equivalent to $\frac{8}{100}$. 0·08GB = $\frac{8}{100}$ GB.

b) The music app requires 0·10 GB.

0·10 is equivalent to $\frac{10}{100}$ or $\frac{1}{10}$ GB.

10 hundredths   1 tenth

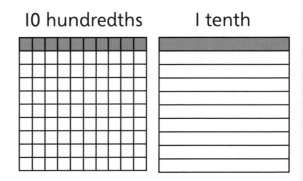

I understood that both $\frac{10}{100}$ and $\frac{1}{10}$ = 0·10 by thinking about exchange.

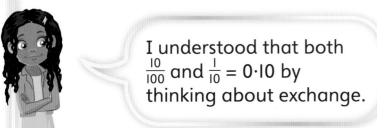

You can write 0·10 as $\frac{1}{10}$ or $\frac{10}{100}$.

Think together

 a) A reading app requires 0·15 GB of memory. Write this as a fraction.

O	•	Tth	Hth
	•	0·1	0·01 0·01 0·01 0·01 0·01

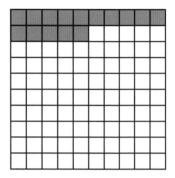

$$0{\cdot}15 \text{ GB} = \frac{\boxed{}}{\boxed{}} \text{ GB}$$

b) Bella's computer has $\frac{17}{100}$ GB memory remaining. Write this as a decimal.

O	•	Tth	Hth
	•		0·01 0·01 0·01 0·01 0·01 0·01 0·01 0·01 0·01 0·01 0·01 0·01 0·01 0·01 0·01 0·01 0·01

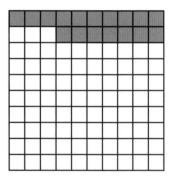

$$\frac{17}{100} \text{ GB} = \boxed{}.\boxed{} \text{ GB}$$

I think sometimes they can be written in more than one way.

2 Write each number as a decimal and as a fraction.

a)

O	•	Tth	Hth
	•	(0·1) (0·1)	(0·01) (0·01) (0·01)

b)

O	•	Tth	Hth
(1)	•	(0·1)	(0·01) (0·01) (0·01) (0·01) (0·01) (0·01) (0·01) (0·01) (0·01) (0·01)

c)

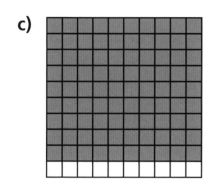

3 Write each of these decimals as both improper fractions and as mixed numbers. The first one has been done for you.

a) 1·27 is equivalent to $\frac{127}{100}$ and $1\frac{27}{100}$

b) 2·32

c) 2·20

d) 1·05

e) 3·5

I remember that I can write 1 whole as $\frac{100}{100}$.

191

→ Practice book 5B p139

Understanding thousandths

Discover

Jamilla

1 **a)** A fraction has been shaded in each of the three diagrams.

Write each as a fraction and as a decimal.

b) Jamilla shades each diagram to show 0·5.

Write this as $\dfrac{}{10}$, $\dfrac{}{100}$ and $\dfrac{}{1,000}$.

Share

a) Each grid represents a whole.

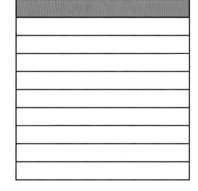

① The whole is split into 10 equal parts.

Each part is $\frac{1}{10}$.

$\frac{1}{10} = 0.1$

② Now each tenth is split into 10 equal parts. There are 100 equal parts.

Each part is $\frac{1}{100}$.

$\frac{1}{100} = 0.01$

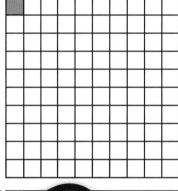

③ Now each hundredth is split into 10 equal parts. There are 1,000 equal parts.

Each part is $\frac{1}{1,000}$.

$\frac{1}{1,000} = 0.001$

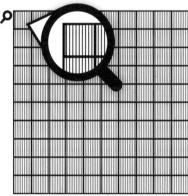

b) 0.5 is equivalent to $\frac{1}{2}$.

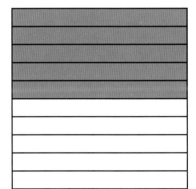 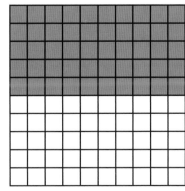 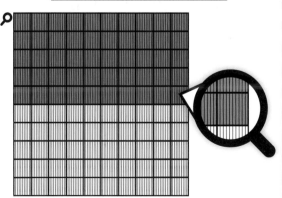

$0.5 = \frac{5}{10}$ $0.5 = \frac{50}{100}$ $0.5 = \frac{500}{1,000}$

Think together

1. Write each shaded area as a fraction and as a decimal.

a)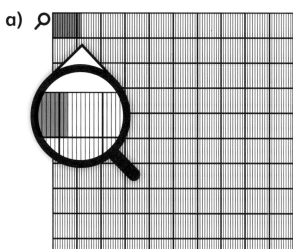

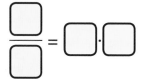

b)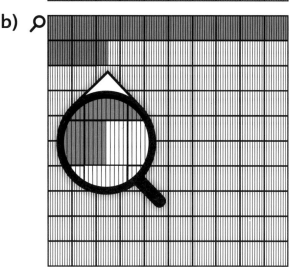

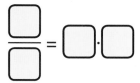

c)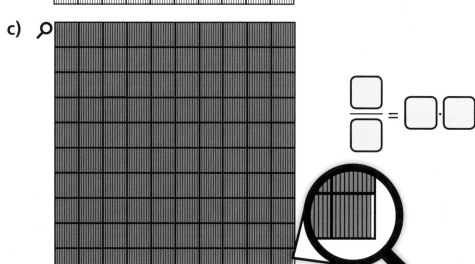

2 Write each of these numbers as a fraction and as a decimal.

a)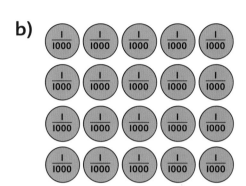

c)

b)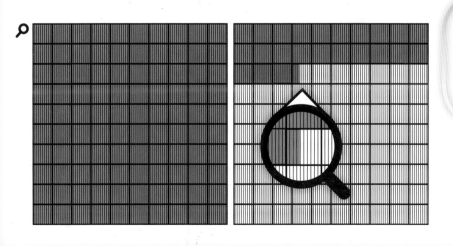

I wonder if I will need to do an exchange.

3 Isla, Aki and Reena have written statements to describe the number 1·234. Who do you think is correct?

CHALLENGE

Isla $\quad 1\frac{234}{1,000} = 1·234$

Aki $\quad \frac{1,234}{1,000} = 1·234$

I will think about what each of the digits in 1·234 represents.

Reena $\quad 1 + \frac{2}{10} + \frac{3}{100} + \frac{4}{1,000} = 1·234$

I will use a diagram to help me work out different ways to write 1·234.

195

→ Practice book 5B p142

Writing thousandths as decimals

Discover

1 **a)** How much flour has Ebo measured?

b) Show this decimal on a place value grid.

Share

a) The scale is marked in hundredths.
The arrow points between 0·12 and 0·13.

I will work out the number by counting.

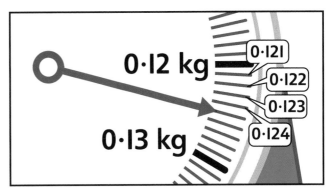

This reminds me of counting up in tenths or hundredths.

Ebo has measured 0·125 kg of flour.

b) 0·125 can be shown on a place value grid like this.

O	•	Tth	Hth	Thth
	•	0·1	0·01 0·01	0·001 0·001 0·001 0·001 0·001

The new column is called the **thousandths** column.
Each counter represents one thousandth ($\frac{1}{1,000}$) in this column.

The number is written as 1 tenth, 2 hundredths and 5 thousandths.

Think together

1 Ebo needs 0·568 litres of milk. Represent this number on a place value grid, and write what each digit represents.

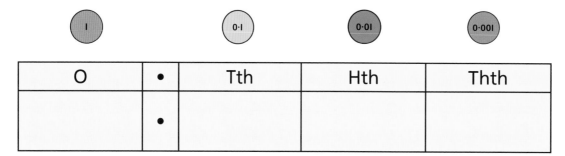

O	•	Tth	Hth	Thth
	•			

The number is written as ☐ tenths, ☐ hundredths, and ☐ thousandths.

2 The recipe needs 0·025 kg of butter.

a) Represent this number on a place value grid.

O	•	Tth	Hth	Thth
	•			

b) Show this number on a number line.

0·02   0·03

c) Say what value each digit in the number represents.

3 Max says he has represented the same number in four different ways.

a) Spot his mistake and show the correction.

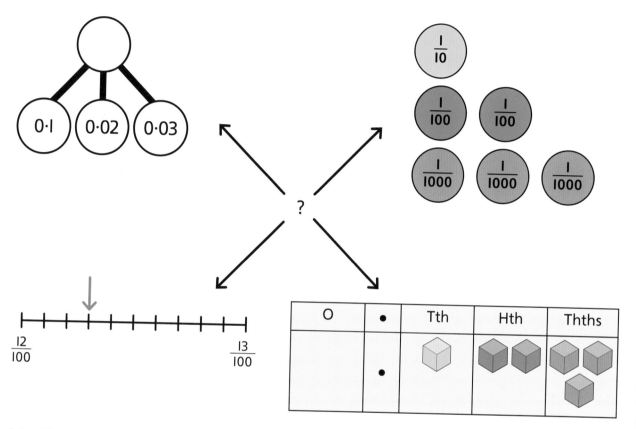

b) Show these numbers using different representations.

0·255

1·205

2·002

2·500

I wonder how many different representations I can make for each number.

199

Ordering and comparing decimals ❶

Discover

RESULTS

Richard: 6·2 cm

Bella: 6·5 cm

Emma: 5·9 cm

The smaller the distance, the quicker the reaction time!

Bella

Emma

Richard

❶ **a)** Order the results from smallest to largest. Who had the quickest reaction time?

b) Convert the decimals to fractions. Use this to check the comparison made in a).

Share

a) The reaction times to compare have digits in the tenths column.

5·9 has the fewest ones, so this is the smallest.

6·2 and 6·5 have the same number of ones, so we look at the tenths.

O	•	Tth
5	•	9
6	•	2
6	•	5

6·2 has the fewest tenths, so this is the next smallest number.

5·9 cm < 6·2 cm < 6·5 cm

The shorter the distance the quicker reaction speed.

I will use a number line to help me compare.

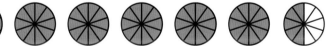

Emma's result was the shortest distance, so she has the quickest reaction time.

b)

        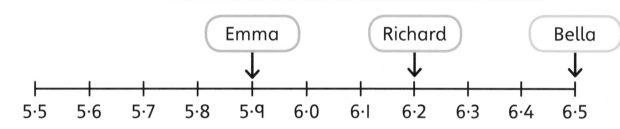

$6·2 = 6\frac{2}{10} = \frac{62}{10}$.
That is **62 tenths**.

$6·5 = 6\frac{5}{10} = \frac{65}{10}$.
That is **65 tenths**.

$5·9 = 5\frac{9}{10} = \frac{59}{10}$.
That is **59 tenths**.

59 tenths is less than 62 tenths which is less than 65 tenths.
59 < 62 < 65

Think together

1 Here are some more reaction time experiment results.

Olivia	Amal	Mo	Lexi
5·1 cm	4·1 cm	5·5 cm	4·0 cm

Order the results from smallest to greatest.

 < ☐ < ☐ < ☐

2 Each diagram represents a decimal. Write them as decimals in a list, from greatest to smallest.

A
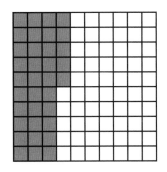

C
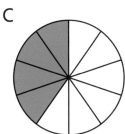

E
$$\frac{28}{100}$$

B
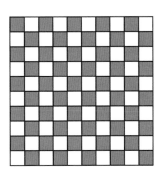

D
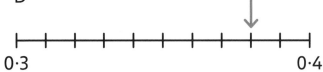

0·3   0·4

I used a place value grid to write my list. I think I can spot a pattern.

3 Ambika, Kate and Max are comparing decimals.

Ambika

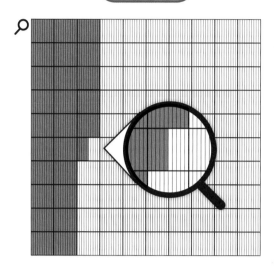

Kate

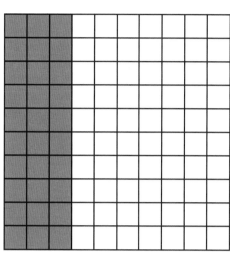

Max **0·24**

Discuss the different methods you can use to compare decimals, and sort the decimals in order of size.

I wonder if it helps to write them all as fractions.

I wrote each number to three decimal places, and then used a place value grid to compare them.

203

Ordering and comparing decimals ❷

Discover

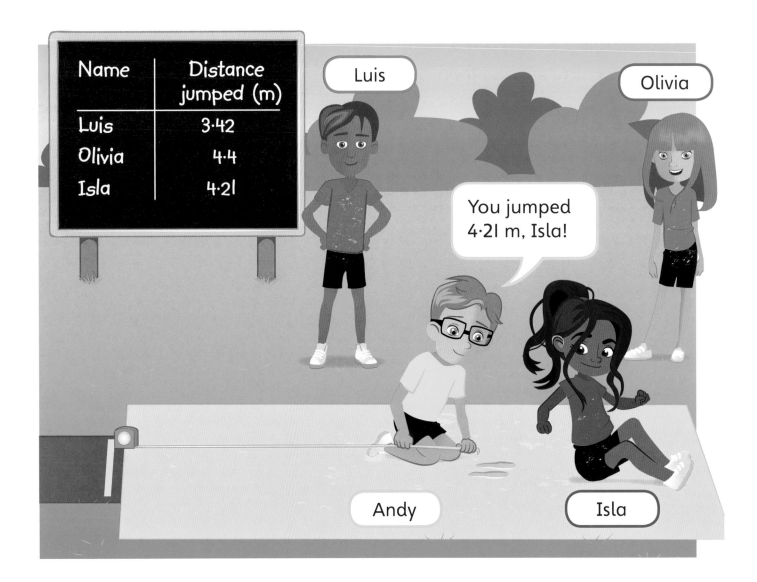

Name	Distance jumped (m)
Luis	3·42
Olivia	4·4
Isla	4·21

Luis

Olivia

You jumped 4·21 m, Isla!

Andy

Isla

❶ **a)** Who is in first place, second place and third place?

b) Andy jumps and is now in second place.

How far could he have jumped?

Share

a) Luis jumps less than 4 m. Luis is in third place.

4·4 m and 4·21 m have a different number of digits.

> I think 4·4 is less than 4·21, because 4 is less than 21.

> I do not think that is right. I will check using counters on a place value grid.

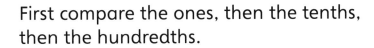

Name	O	•	Tth	Hth
Luis	① ① ①	•	⓪·¹ ⓪·¹ ⓪·¹ ⓪·¹	⓪·⁰¹ ⓪·⁰¹
Olivia	① ① ① ①	•	⓪·¹ ⓪·¹ ⓪·¹ ⓪·¹	
Isla	① ① ① ①	•	⓪·¹ ⓪·¹	⓪·⁰¹

First compare the ones, then the tenths, then the hundredths.

Both numbers have 4 ones, but 4·4 has more tenths than 4·21.

> Start comparing from the column with the largest place value.

$3·42 < 4·21 < 4·4$

Luis is in third place, Isla is in second place, Olivia is in first place.

b) A decimal number line helps to show the possible distances that Andy could have jumped.

3rd place ↓   2nd place ↓   1st place ↓

3·4   3·5   3·6   3·7   3·8   4   4·1   4·2   4·3   4·4   4·5

Andy's jump could be any distance between 4·21 m and 4·40 m.

Think together

1 Here are the results from the 200 m sprint.

Use a place value grid to order the times from slowest to fastest.

Runner	Time
A	21·49 s
B	21·30 s
C	21·07 s
D	21·09 s
E	21·04 s

O	•	Tth	Hth
	•		
	•		
	•		
	•		
	•		

Slowest to fastest runners: ▢ > ▢ > ▢ > ▢ > ▢

2 A competition shot put is supposed to weigh 7·26 kg.

4 shot put balls have been weighed. Which ones are too heavy, which are too light and which are the correct weight?

A

7·258 kg

B

7·3 kg

C

7·199 kg

D
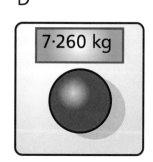
7·260 kg

3 Write a number that fits each description.

a) Any number between 4 and 4·1.

```
├─────────────────────────────────────┤
4                                    4·1
```

b) Any number between 4·59 and 4·6.

```
├─────────────────────────────────────┤
4·59                                 4·6
```

c) A fraction that is greater than 0·6 and less than 0·61.

I will use a place value grid with counters to check my ideas.

I will convert the decimals into fractions to help.

207

Rounding decimals

Discover

1 a) Do you agree with Jen that all of the boxes weigh approximately 9 kg?

Round each weight to the nearest whole number.

b) A fifth box rounds to 9 kg. What could it weigh?

Share

a) Each of the four boxes weighs between 9 kg and 10 kg.

To round to the nearest whole number, work out if it is nearer to 9 or nearer to 10.

I drew a number line and marked it in tenths. Now I can see that 9·2 and 9·3 are nearer to 9, and 9·8 is nearer to 10. But what about 9·5?

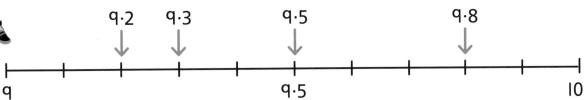

9·5 is exactly half-way between 9 and 10. The half-way number always rounds up.

9·2 and 9·3 round to 9 kg to the nearest whole number.

9·5 and 9·8 round to 10 kg to the nearest whole number.

b) 8·5 rounds to 9, but 9·5 rounds to 10. The box could weigh from 8·5 kg up to 9·49 kg.

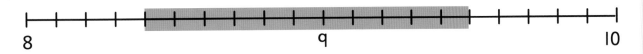

Think together

1 Round each decimal number to the nearest whole number.

a) 1·9   c) 0·9   e) 1·09

b) 4·4   d) 2·5   f) 0·25

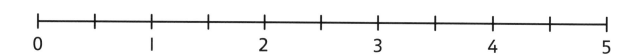

```
├──┼──┼──┼──┼──┼──┼──┼──┼──┼──┤
0     1     2     3     4     5
```

2 Round each of these numbers to one decimal place.

O	•	Tth	Hth
3	•	5	6
2	•	0	9
0	•	2	2
5	•	0	0

We say numbers like 1·2 or 23·5 have **one decimal place**.

Numbers like 1·35 and 10·79 have **two decimal places**.

I understand it more deeply when I draw a number line.

I can tell which numbers will round up or down by looking at the hundredths digit.

3 **a)** Round 1·24 to the nearest whole number.

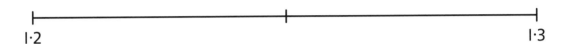

1   2

b) Round 1·24 to the nearest tenth.

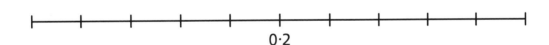

1·2   1·3

c) A number rounds to 0·2 to the nearest tenth.

What could the number have been?

0·2

I will also try using a place value grid to help with the rounding.

Rounding to the nearest tenth can be called 'rounding to one decimal place', because the rounded number will not have any hundredths.

211

Understanding percentages

Discover

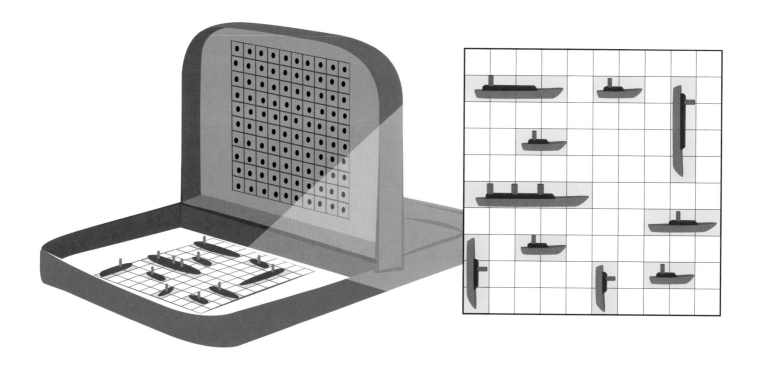

1 a) Reena has placed her ships on the grid.

How much of the grid is covered?

How much of the grid is empty?

b) She removes these two ships.

Now how much of the grid is covered and how much is empty?

Share

I moved the ships side by side to make it easier to work out.

a) The grid is 10 rows of 10 squares.

$10 \times 10 = 100$

There are 100 squares in total.

The ships cover 29 out of 100 squares.

$100 - 29 = 71$

So 71 squares out of 100 are not covered.

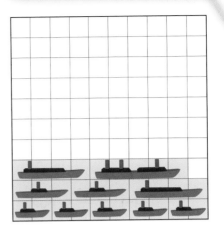

Percentages can describe this situation.

29% of the grid is covered.

71% of the grid is empty.

Per cent (%) means 'parts out of 100'. So 1 per cent means 1 part out of 100 or $\frac{1}{100}$. 10 per cent means 10 parts out of 100 or $\frac{10}{100}$.

b) The two ships covered $4 + 3 = 7$ squares.

$29 - 7 = 22$

So now only 22 out of 100 are covered.

22% of the grid is covered.

$100 - 22 = 78$

So now 78 out of 100 squares are uncovered.

78% of the grid is empty.

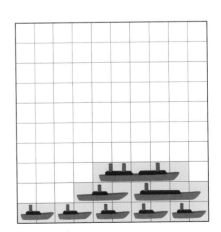

Think together

1 What percentage is shaded in these diagrams?

a)

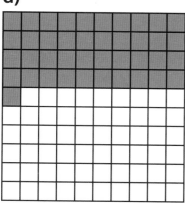

b)

c)

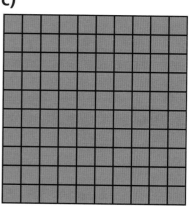

In one of these hundredths grids the whole is shaded. I wonder if that is 1%.

2 Each of the pictures represents a percentage.

Which one is the odd one out?

A

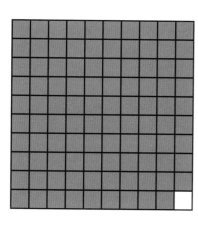

B

C

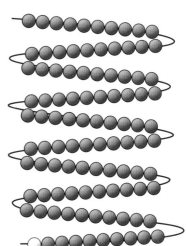

3 **a)** Emma and Zac are discussing 1% and 100%. Do you agree with Emma or Zac?

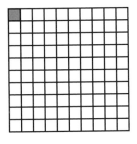 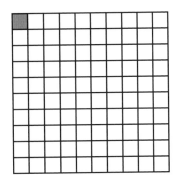 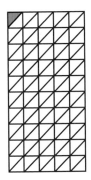

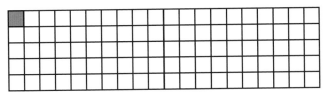

These all show different percentages, because they are different shapes and sizes.

Emma

No, I think these all show the same percentage. Each percent looks different because each whole is a different shape or size.

Zac

b) Max has drawn a diagram. He says it shows 1%. Do you agree?

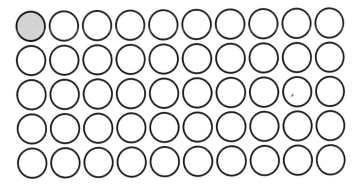

→ **Practice book 5B p157**

Percentages as fractions and decimals

Discover

Jamilla

1 **a)** Find two sets of three matching cards.

b) Write a fraction and draw a diagram to match the remaining card.

Share

a) Card D shows 28 squares shaded out of 100. This can be written as 28% (Card A) and as $\frac{28}{100}$ (Card G).

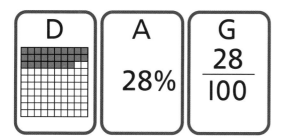

I will start with the diagram cards.

Each shows 100 equal parts. This represents hundredths.

Card F shows 2 squares shaded out of 100. This can be written as 2% (Card E) and as $\frac{2}{100}$. $\frac{2}{100}$ is the 2 hundredths which is equivalent to the decimal 0·02 (Card B).

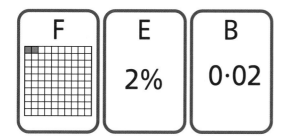

b) The remaining card is Card C, which shows 22%.

22% is 22 equal parts out of 100 and so can be written as $\frac{22}{100}$.

This can be represented on a hundredths grid like this:

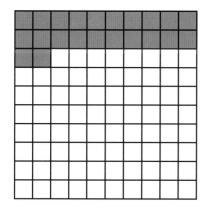

We can say 22% = $\frac{22}{100}$. The percentage and the fraction are equivalent.

Think together

1 Write the numbers represented by each diagram as a fraction, decimal and percentage.

a)

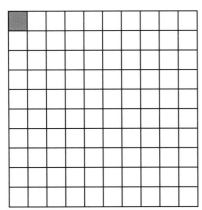

b)

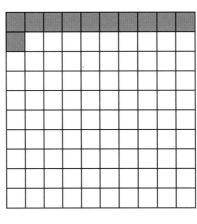

c)

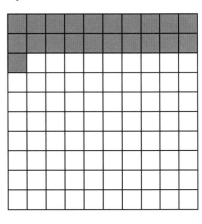

2 Complete the table to show the equivalent fractions, decimals and percentages.

70% $\frac{12}{100}$ 5%   0·09 $\frac{5}{100}$ 0·7   9%   0·12

Fraction	Decimal	Percentage
$\frac{9}{100}$	☐	☐
☐	0·05	☐
☐	☐	12%
$\frac{70}{100}$	☐	☐

3 **a)** Ambika and Richard are talking about saving their pocket money.

I have saved 100% of my pocket money.

I have saved 100% of mine. We must have saved the same!

Ambika

Richard

Explain why Richard could be wrong.

b) Ambika wants to convert 100% into a decimal.

Show how to write 100% as a decimal.

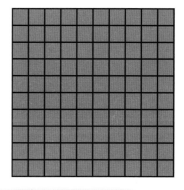

I think it could be 0·100.

I do not think that is right. 100% means 100 hundredths.

219

Equivalent fractions, decimals and percentages

Discover

Luis

1 **a)** Look at the pegboard in front of Luis. What fraction, percentage and decimal of the board is covered by circle pegs?

What fraction, percentage and decimal of the board is covered by square pegs?

b) What fraction, percentage and decimal of the board is covered by triangle pegs?

220

Share

a) The circle pegs fill 10 out of 100.

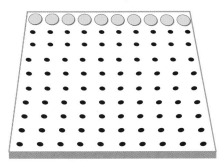

They fill 1 row out of 10.

$\frac{1}{10} = 0.1$

$\frac{10}{100} = 10\%$

$\frac{10}{100} = \frac{1}{10}$

$\frac{1}{10}$, 10% or 0.1 of the board is covered by circle pegs.

> I can say that $\frac{1}{10}$ is equivalent to 10% or 0.1.

The square pegs fill 30 out of 100. They fill 3 rows out of 10.

$\frac{3}{10}$ is equivalent to 30% or 0.3.

$\frac{3}{10}$, 30% or 0.3 of the board is covered by square pegs.

b) The triangle pegs are in 6 rows of 5.

$6 \times 5 = 30$

That is 30 pegs out of 100.

$\frac{30}{100} = \frac{3}{10} = 0.3 = 30\%$

$\frac{3}{10}$, 30% or 0.3 of the board is covered by triangle pegs.

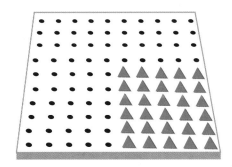

> It is still $\frac{3}{10}$, even though it is not 3 full rows.

Think together

1 Convert these decimals, fractions and percentages to complete the table.

Decimal	0·1	0·2	☐	☐	☐	1	0
Tenths	$\frac{1}{10}$	☐	☐	$\frac{8}{10}$	☐	☐	☐
Hundredths	$\frac{10}{100}$	☐	☐	☐	$\frac{90}{100}$	☐	☐
Percentage	10%	☐	40%	☐	☐	☐	☐

2 What fraction, decimal and percentage is shaded?

a)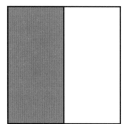

b)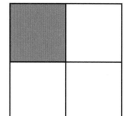

c)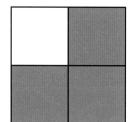

These diagrams are not split into 100 equal parts. I wonder how to find the percentages.

I will think about how I can describe the amount shaded.

3 **a)** Andy and Reena both took a test. Reena scored 30 out of 60. Andy scored 30%.

How can you compare their scores?

I will think about Reena's score as a fraction.

I can convert Reena's score to a percentage.

b) Emma has 40 marbles. 4 are blue.

What percentage are blue?

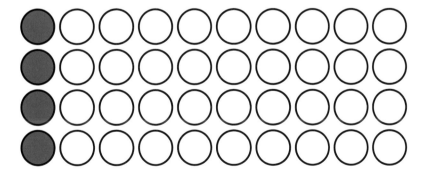

223

End of unit check

1 Which fraction is represented in the place value grid?

O	•	Tth
0	•	3

A $\frac{3}{10}$ **B** $\frac{10}{3}$ **C** $\frac{3}{100}$ **D** $\frac{1}{3}$

2 Which decimal is shown?

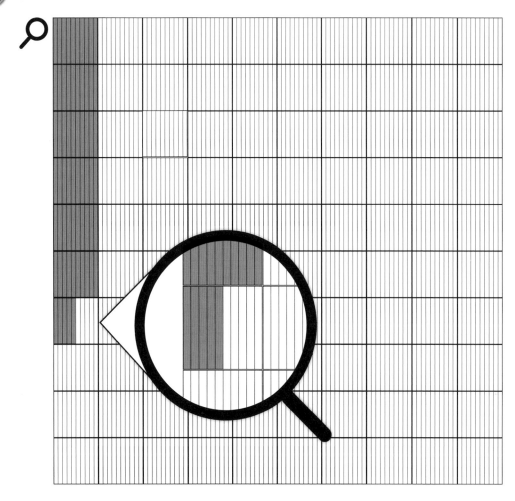

A 0·65   **B** 6·5   **C** 0·065   **D** 1·650

3 Which number would complete the statement correctly?

3·802 > ☐

A 3·9   **B** 3·81   **C** 3·8   **D** 4

4 What is 9·55 rounded to the nearest tenth?

A 9·5   **B** 9·65   **C** 10   **D** 9·6

5 Which pair is represented here?

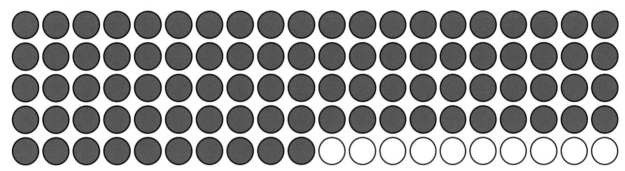

A 0·9 and 9%

B $\frac{9}{100}$ and 90%

C 80% and $\frac{8}{10}$

D 90% and 0·9

6 Put these fractions, decimals and percentages in order from smallest to greatest.

0·3   13% $\frac{31}{100}$ 0·04 $\frac{2}{10}$ $\frac{130}{1,000}$

Smallest ☐ ☐ ☐ ☐ ☐ ☐ Greatest

225

→ Practice book 5B p166

There were lots of new things to learn. Sometimes I made mistakes but I will keep trying until I get it right!

Remember there is often more than one way to solve a problem. Look for other methods.

I enjoy listening to my partners to learn from them.

It is great to share ideas!

What have we learnt?

Can you do all these things?

- ⚡ Compare and order fractions
- ⚡ Add and subtract fractions
- ⚡ Multiply fractions
- ⚡ Write decimals as fractions
- ⚡ Understand percentages

Some of it was difficult, but we did not give up!

Now you are ready for the next books!

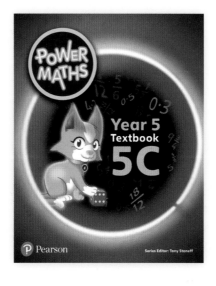